CHANGING WOMAN AND HER SISTERS

CHANGING WOMAN AND HER SISTERS

Feminine Aspects of Selves and Deities

By Sheila Moon

Guild for Psychological Studies
Publishing House
San Francisco, California

Published in the United States of America by
The Guild for Psychological Studies Publishing House
2230 Divisadero Street
San Francisco, California 94115

Grateful acknowledgment is made to the following for permission to reprint selections from the works indicated
below:
    The lines from "The Invocation to Kali" and from "My
Sisters, O My Sisters" from *Collected Poems, 1930-1973*, by
May Sarton, are reprinted by permission of W.W. Norton &
Company Copyright ©1974 by May Sarton.
    The lines from *Coming of Age*, by Babette Deutsch, In-
diana University Press, 1959, are reprinted by permission
of Adam Yarmolinsky, Washington, D.C.

Grateful acknowledgment is made to the following for
their contribution to this book:
Susan Renfrew — Cover Design
Marilyn Robertson — Photograph

Typesetting by Pan Typesetters, Eugene, Oregon
Printing by Braun-Brumfield, Inc., Ann Arbor, Michigan

Library of Congress Cataloging in Publication Data

Moon, Sheila, 1910 -
    Changing Woman and Her Sisters

    Bibliography: p. 222
    1. Navajo Indians—Religion and mythology. 2. Pueblo In-
dians—Religion and mythology. 3. Femininity (Psychology)
4. Femininity of God. 5. Psychoanalysis. 6. Indians of North
America—Southwest, New—Religion and mythology. I.
Title.
E99.N3M67   1985   299'.72   84-27901

ISBN   0-917479-02-5   casebound
ISBN   0-917479-03-3   paperback

To all the many seminar members
and colleagues and analysands
who have made this book a reality.

TABLE OF CONTENTS

I.

Introduction

WHAT?

Changing Woman and Her Sisters is the story of a land and its earliest people, of the beauty of this land, of the mystery of its first inhabitants, and of the richness of the stories told by those early comers — stories still told in the cere-monials and rituals of the Native Americans who live on the land and enrich it. *Changing Woman and Her Sisters* is also, and primarily, the telling of the Feminine in creations — and such a telling as is unique in creation and origin stories.

These Native American myths of the Feminine goddesses are exceedingly powerful and important for American women. (And men also.) American women, of all the world's women, probably play more roles and are more culturally variegated than most others. Therefore the many facets that each of the myths expresses, and the complexity of interrelation-ships delineated, are unusual and unusually helpful for the contemporary woman called to play many roles without becoming fragmented.

The major portion of the mythic material has been taken from the many chants and accompanying myths of the Navajo people.* Also, a goodly number of tales and ceremonial accompaniments from the Pueblo people — especially Hopi, Acoma, and Zuni — is included for added dimensions and comparisons. Both Navajo and Pueblo people are highly gifted artistically, as story tellers and as healers.

The Navajo are more individualistic than the Pueblo people. The Navajo came to this continent later than did the Pueblo peoples and apparently borrowed from the Pueblo myths, giving their own added vitality and thrust to the tales. Each Pueblo village and clan has its own version of the various myths. In the same way, each Navajo "singer" or "chanter" has a singular version of whatever myth is part of a chant.

The singularity of these tales is particularly meaningful for our time of history, because our time is particularly one of masses of people rather than of individuals. These myths stress the needs of individuals, the hurts and healings of individuals from within the songs and chants of each mythic tale.

---

*Henderson says of myth that it "is the exteriorized self-portrayal of the inner psychic world" (33) and this is what this text will be setting forth via the Indian myths.

WHY?

For reasons not fully understood by me, I have been drawn to American Indian cultures since my grade school days. I can recall the irritation of one teacher (and there were probably others) because I would not draw or paint any other subjects except Indians and scenes from Indian life as I imagined them to be. I read all the books I could get about Indians.

This deep and unexplained interest was clearly manifested in the way in which I discovered the Navajo myths. I was a teaching assistant in psychology at the University of California at Berkeley, living on a very small salary and working for my Ph.D. degree. I went only rarely to San Francisco because it was too costly. On one such occasion I visited my favorite bookshop and saw on a counter display a beautiful book on the Navajo *Emergence myth*. Its price was exactly one tenth of my monthly salary. On three separate occasions during the next month I visited this shop. The book kept being there. So I bought it on the third trip, feeling extravagant and foolish and wasteful and very happy.

In a few months I had read the book several times and was deeply moved and fascinated by it. I decided to use it in my teaching. It was exciting to see how deeply people responded, how newly it helped them to open themselves to their inner being and to understand inner problems and resolutions. The myth communicated much better than textbooks.

Some years later, when I was studying in Zurich in Jungian psychology at the Institute, I had the opportunity to work through some of this Indian material with Mrs. Linda Fierz-David. Her intuitive-feeling insights added greatly to my own understandings and to the richness of psychological insights in these myths. I also had some time with Dr. Von Franz on similar material and am grateful for her interest and ideas.

Another of my answers to the "Why?" is the fact that our planet, so trivial in galactic immensities, is all that we have to live on. Our treatment of this home is slowly destroying it. There are also my siblings everywhere of all colors and conditions, suffering from wealth, poverty, war, obesity, hunger, heart attacks, starvation, insanity, loneliness, suicide, indifference, power. And they have so few real roots to help them to grow deeper.

Because I care about this planet home, and about myself (inward and outward), and about my multitude of siblings (inward and outward), I am concerned that we try to restore a better balance in ourselves and on our planet between the opposites necessary for psychological and spiritual health. Unless we can do this, we and our planet home have a high chance of becoming nonexistent. And that seems to me a terrible waste of a grave and perhaps unique experiment.

As a psychotherapist, novelist, poet, mythologist, and person who dreams, I am therefore wanting us not to waste anywhere. I want to emphasize wholeness rather than fragmentation. I care about that great mystery, a whole person, as different from that fragmented person which most of us tend to become. Whole persons are changing persons — changing used in the sense of growing, expanding — used in the opposite of stasis. In the same way a whole society can be distinguished from an alienated society — or even, if you will, a whole planet from a fragmented and anguished one. Whole in the way of encompassing archetypal opposites.

Still another reason why is that the human psyche — struggling to articulate evolving images of the individual, the gods, Godhead, illness, misfortune and healing — weaves its myths from inside its own fruitful ground of dream. If the psyche is a living thing, an intrinsic part of human creativity and meaning, then the myth is, as a dream is, a living thing in the psyche related to where the human species evolutionarily is. The species and the dreams and myths of the species cooperate to spin the fine strong thread of true Becoming.

It is important to realize that "primitive" or "simple" people are neither primitive nor simple where the inner structure of the psyche is concerned. They have the complexities of the less primitive but do not always have the advanced ways of expressing these complexities. So when hardships come, as illness or bad times, they turn to the ways of singing, chanting, performing the ancient rituals, telling the ancient tales told to them by parents, grandparents, elders of the group to which they belong. Such tales and songs have endured because they have been helpful and meaningful, and can be said to spring from the archetypal foundations of the human being. This is the root of folktales and chants and ritual plantings and repeated rites and words of magic and individual dreams.

This undergirding of the human being is the basis of all myths and rites connected with myths, and chants connected with rites and myths. And songs. And ritual dance. And the making of fetishes. And the making of sand-paintings. And the long learning and skill of the Navajo medicine man or medicine woman.

If any one of you has ever watched a very small child sitting alone, placing pebbles in a particular way, singing softly to itself certain invented words over and over, and have seen the peace come into the child's face — and the joy — you have seen in its most simple form the source of the myths and chants and rituals of adult humans.

Mythic complexes such as will be dealt with here have assisted the Navajo and Pueblo people for generations to keep and to use their meanings, no matter what exigencies of fortune and misfortune come to them. If we non-Indian people can dare to interiorize such helpful symbolisms and take them as seriously as we well might take our dreams, they can help heal us.

Why is the Feminine stressed? Because I believe it is the more neglected, rejected, and misunderstood of the Masculine/Feminine opposites operative in all of us. It is thus the most needful of our understanding if we are to regain our balance. Modern women struggling to identify themselves can relate to this Feminine as the archetypal She appears in these stories. She can sharpen definitions and bring a broadened spectrum of dimensions. Modern men also need this She.

HOW?

Over a long period of time I have worked my way through the marvelous variety and challenge of these various myths of the Feminine deities. I feel that each of them presents to us ways to understand and relate to the multiform and much-needed Feminine principle. No matter if we are female or male, we need to learn about, feel into, bring into reality, the many-sided She. Our white culture has been for so many centuries dominated by the Masculine that we have lost touch with the Feminine in its deepest sense.

This pair — the Feminine and the Masculine — are contained in each mote of humankind and also in the images of the Other. Even Genesis 1:27 states that Yahweh made humans "in *our* image," male and female created he them. This plural points to the fact that, in Hebrew, the word translated as "man" (*adam*) is a plural word meaning male and female, or humankind. The implication is that Yahweh is also plural.

Modern women and men need to hear this. They need also to realize that these two psychic energy sources, Feminine and Masculine, live in each human being and must be permitted — indeed, encouraged — to function more equally or else part of the personality wastes away. Dr. Jung's work has greatly illuminated these two archetypal principles and forces as co-equal, and as necessary to each person as inhale-exhale, or two-handedness, or bipolar cortex.*

I have taken Feminine mythic characters from Navajo and Pueblo sources, placed them in a sequence which seemed most grounding for our understanding and for their symbolic psychological meanings, and then discussed them both mythically and psychologically. I have added examples from my psychological practice of over twenty-five years. The examples, I hope, will help others to realize how to work with the mythic symbols as relevant to their own inner worlds.

---

*C.G. Jung defined the archetypes as irrepresentable inner dispositions to actions made evident through their effects in images and ideas. He said that "archetypes are present in the unconscious as potential abilities which, at a given moment, are realized and applied when brought into consciousness by a creative act" (72, p. 22). He then added that the "archetypal primordial forms were already present . . . at the dawn of human consciousness." Jung postulated a two-layered unconscious, so to speak — one part composed of material which had its origin in the specific life of the specific individual, and this he called the "personal unconscious." The other part was a given, virtually a genetic inheritance of patterns of response to usual situations. It was related to "instinct" of the lower animal form. For a complete description and discussion of these aspects, the reader is referred to primary material. See Bibliography for details.

Cirlot (15, pp. xxxiv, xxxv) has a concise and beautiful description of the archetypes as Jung saw them in relationship to the collective unconscious. He ends his description with these words. "Archetypes are like all-embracing parables: their meaning is only partially accessible."

WHO?

Navajos and Pueblos. But what does that mean? Who are they? The Pueblos and the Navajos doubtless were part of various migrations in ages past when people came from the Bering Sea area and across the frozen straits — following game perhaps, or/and hunting for a better place to live. The Navajo people, as comparative latecomers, called the Pueblo people "Anasazi" — the Old Ones.

Going backward in time, the Anasazi culture dates from roughly 800 A.D. The Anasazi culture is predated by the early Basketmaker culture, about 1500 B.C., and by a so-called Mogollon culture, from roughly 2000 B.C. And behind these cultures are the remains of villages, cliff dwellings, cave homes, pictographs and petroglyphs scattered throughout the Southwest in places such as Mesa Verde, Chaco Canyon, Canyon de Chelly, Monument Valley.

The Pueblo peoples do not speak a common language. The Zuni have a language unrelated to any known language — perhaps a composite. The Hopi speak a Shoshonean language. The Acoma and other Rio Grande Pueblo groups speak Keresan. (The name "Pueblo" was given them collectively by the Spanish when they came into the Southwest seeking golden treasure.) The Pueblo peoples live communally, in many-roomed dwellings clustered together, usually on high mesas.

The facts that three root languages are spoken by the Pueblo people and that they are distributed through the Southwest in several unique and relatively separated communities, give a different flavor to their mythic tellings. The Hopi people have seemed, to more than one investigator, "secret." It was not until the 1960's that Frank Waters worked with their leading people and helped them to record most of their important myths. Waters describes them as a peaceful people, ancient, caring for their earth passionately, beginning to resent the domination of a technological society. The small Zuni republic is still intact after four centuries. Acoma, farthest south of the Pueblos, survives with upward of a thousand people.

The Navajo language is related to the Athabaskan, the same language spoken by certain Eskimo groups. This fact, together with the Oriental facial shape of the Navajo, places them definitely in the Asiatic migrant group. They have been part of the Southwest cultures at least as far back as 1000 A.D., and probably considerably longer. They incorporate aspects of Eskimo culture and parts of Pueblo culture. They do not live communally but in separate family dwellings scattered widely throughout their lands. These dwellings — hogans, as they are called — are wonderfully adapted to the lonely life in harsh country.

The Navajo are a people of observable physical vigor and great psychological stamina. They have absorbed into their mythic system aspects of other systems. They imaginatively enriched such myths as they have "borrowed." And they have survived persecutory treatment for generations. Today their population is on the increase despite the impoverished land on which they live.

Very recently I was in the Navajo country and had the opportunity for a long and easy discussion with a middle-aged Navajo man about the various "chants" (or "ways") still being given by medicine men or women for purposes of mental and physical healings. It was good to hear that many of them are still extant — although there are fewer Navajo chanters and healers who know them and can give them.

Herding, weaving, and agriculture have been at the core of Navajo life for a very long time. They remain so. Many of the Navajo still move with their flocks from canyon bottoms to valleys and mesas with the changing seasons. Pickup trucks have replaced horse-and-wagon transportation. Some Navajos have employment outside the reservation. But there are still medicine men and women and chants and "sings" and weaving and healing. And their austerely lovely dry paintings (sand or pollen), the ceremonies for healing, for puberty, for cleansing, remain as testaments of the evolving of a primitive migrating group into one with its own unique and relatively stable identity.

On this same trip, I visited the Zuni Pueblo and the Hopi Mesa villages. It is sad to realize that the Hopi people are very slowly moving away from the past. The old mesa villages, high and lovely above the valley floor, are crumbling. At Zuni the earliest pueblo is a ruin, almost undiscoverable, and the Zuni people live in a small modern village. But both groups still keep their ritual year — at least in part — and both groups continue to carve and ornament their kachina figures. These latter are doll-sized representations of the great masked divinity figures which appear in their various festivals.

Mythic material from Hopi, Zuni, and Acoma Pueblo groups is to be found more frequently in earlier anthropological writings appearing in such journals as *American Folk-lore* or U.S. Bureau of Ethnology publications. In recent years, however, Frank Waters prevailed upon Hopi elders to tell their myths for all people to read — truly a fine work. (87A) Courlander also brought out a book of Hopi myths told by Hopi tribal leaders. (17)

Mythic material from the Navajo is full and rich and has been extensively recorded. Many people have been captured by the loveliness of the sand paintings and the mystery of the great chants, which are given almost always for individuals rather than for the group. Because the Navajos are individualistic rather than communal, this affects their rituals and their art forms. (That is, a sand painting is wiped away as soon as a ritual ends.) By contrast, for example, Kachina masks are kept in the secret rooms (kivas) of a Pueblo group clan from one year to the next and used over and over.

Both Navajo and Pueblo myths reveal in certain aspects some possible relationship to Mesoamerican myths, i.e., their four dimensionality of colors and directions. And this in its own turn reveals possible links to Asian systems. Some anthropologists have also hinted at Pacific Islands roots. Proof is lacking as yet, however.

Because the bulk of my material is taken from the Navajo, a few further words about these people are needed. For the Navajo, the supernatural powers, good and evil, affect all of life. (This is differently true for the Pueblo people.) These powers are the Holy People, holy "in the meaning of powerful and mysterious, of belonging to the sacred as opposed to the profane world." (49, p. 122) At the same time, Navajo mythic characters are very human in behavior and characteristics, and the inner human problems are set forth.

Some years ago I was privileged to exchange letters with Herbert Blatchford, an outstanding leader and educator among the Navajo people. The great myths of the Navajo, he said — in answer to questions from me — involve a true spiritual process and do relate to the inner being. The four-foldness contained in the myths is "taken from the rhythm of nature." He also wrote that "because of his belief in harmony and in following the natural course of events, the Navajo Indian does not project his aims and aspirations far into the distant future, but rather thinks in terms of the present and the past so as not to disrupt the blessedness of harmony."

Navajo social structure and Navajo ritual are barely separable — a fact which is also true for Pueblos, for most so-called "primitive" cultures, and was true for many earlier "high" cultures such as those of Babylon, Egypt, Mayan, and Mesoamerica. In a society in which individuals are not separate fragments but interconnected "particles" cohering to form the society and to shape it, myths and rituals are binding agents.

The separate individuals are held by the rituals which arise from the unconscious levels of the society itself.

The "sacred" and "secular" aspects of such cultures are very difficult to differentiate. This is true of Navajo and Pueblo culture to a remarkable degree even now — or until very recent years — despite the assaults on it by non-Indians for generations. The various chants and rituals and tellings of the related myths are deeply embedded in daily life. The chants are concerned with healing of mind and body and are thus involved in keeping life in balance, harmonious, "in beauty."

In their book on the Navajo, Kluckhohn and Leighton (49, p. 223f) list the following basic premises of Navajo "philosophy": (1) "Life is very, very dangerous." (2) "Nature is more powerful than man." (3) "The personality is a whole." (4) "Respect the integrity of the individual." (5) "Everything exists in two parts, the male and the female, which belong together and complete each other." (6) "Human nature is neither good nor evil — both qualities are blended in all persons from birth on." (7) "Like produces like and the part stands for the whole." (8) "What is said is to be taken literally." (9) "This life is what counts."

These basic insights express much that the non-Indian has yet to heed regarding what can and cannot be done to natural things, or what needs to be assumed about human nature, or what are the rights of any individual.

Particularly essential for our present study

are (5) and (7) — (5) because it emphasizes how basic the Feminine is in Navajo life and thought, and (7) because it provides the undergirding for the symbolic meanings in the Navajo myths to be dealt with subsequently. I would also stress (6), in order to point out that the Navajo definition of evil or sin is what occurs when things are out of order. We will return to this in later chapters.

It is necessary and valuable to learn the actual roles of women in Navajo culture. Gladys Reichard (76), in one of the definitive studies of the Navajo, has provided an extensive survey of both the Navajo woman's position and of the Feminine in general.

The Navajo trace family relationships through the female line — and thus the woman is in a position of considerable authority. There are and have been respected women chanters — a healing wisdom ("priestly") role which in most cultures is held only by men. The girl at her puberty rites becomes an honored symbol of tribal fecundity and its religious power. Partly because of this, certain restrictions are placed upon the woman, although she is held equal to men economically, socially, politically.

Reichard says that "once strengthened by ritual, a woman may undertake and withstand anything a man can." (76, p. 172) Moreover, the individual in charge of the important rattle stick in the highly masculine War Ceremony "should be a reliable female virgin." Navajo women have been singers of the *Night Chant*, handling the masks which are central symbols of that great ritual.

In her book *Spider Woman* (77), Reichard reports of the case of a woman who left her husband because she believed he had been seeing another woman. Her family took the case before a Navajo judge in the employ of the United States government, and were given full support in presenting the situation from the wife's point of view. This is not unusual. The man's rights are no more protected than are the woman's.

Years ago I had the great good fortune, when I was in Santa Fe, N.M. working on Navajo material at the Navajo museum, to meet Fr. Berard Haile, one of the outstanding and central persons who worked with the Navajo. He had been critically ill and was in the hospital when I saw him. I was led into his room by an Indian nurse. He was a small man, and even smaller because of his illness. His eyes are the eyes of a gnome, I thought, as I approached the bed where he was curled. He lifted a frail hand in greeting, and then reached under his pillow and pulled out a half-smoked cigar.

"The nurse doesn't like this," he said with an impish smile. "Don't let her know." And he lighted his cigar. "So what can I tell you?"

For about a half hour we talked. I asked questions about some of the material I had been reading in the museum — some of his manuscripts and some from other specialists. He answered carefully and thoughtfully. He corrected some of his colleagues for being too prudish and therefore for not translating Navajo words correctly. He also described to me the great overall *Blessingway*. He said that it began with emergence out of the third world of creation (the world of 12 words) with Changing Woman, who is also Turquoise Woman, Abalone Woman, and Jet Woman. What he was saying was that the Goddess carried the full weight of the four-fold Navajo directions, colors, and sacred stones.

From this brief but cherished meeting I received a sense of the richness of the Feminine in all Navajo myths and rituals and customs. Fr. Berard's words were echoed in words of Washington Matthews (57), another of the great students of the Navajo:

> I have only this to say of the Navajo woman, she is the most independent woman under the sun. She is master of all her own property. Marriage alienates nothing from her. Divorce is in her hands as well as in her husband's. Her family is her own. . . . A favorite fiction of sociologists is that the condition of women improves in a direct ratio with the advance of civilization. Be not deceived, oh sisters, go to the savage wife of the Arizona deserts and learn something of her.

Kluckhohn and Leighton's point (5), given earlier, is relevant here: "Everything exists in two parts, the male and the female, which belong together and complete each other." This runs like a leitmotif through Navajo myths and chants, giving them a particular sense of balance between Feminine and Masculine opposites. These two dimensions are *not* synonymous with woman and man in Navajo thought.

Washington Matthews observed that the Navajo distinction is "between that which is coarser, rougher, and more violent, called male . . . and that which is finer, weaker, and more gentle, called female. . . ." He also pointed out that this is beyond a differentiation of sexes, "since two deities of the same sex may be paired and perform the same kinds of functions as do male and female in other cases. Therefore, in ceremonies the underlying symbolism must be understood." (57) Potency, mobility, energy, bigness, and dominance are male; and generative capacity, passive power, endurance, smallness, and compliance are female.

Because the Feminine is honored in all its aspects in Navajo myth and religious ritual, a wide dimensionality is offered which is rarely found in mythic systems. (Closest to it is Pueblo, from whom almost surely the Navajo borrowed.)

The Navajo mythic complex has been my paradigm for understanding the Feminine in contemporary individuals and in our society, as well as in divinity. Feminine mythic characters can be, as I have already said, of either sex. However, because myths (and dreams) generally use images in a quite straightforward and almost simplistic fashion to get their "thought" across, female figures are the carriers par excellence of the Feminine. Not the *only* carriers, but the majority. Female "holy ones" in Navajo and Pueblo myth are divinizations of Feminine attributes.

The psyches of modern men and women respond to such Feminine carriers eagerly — as I shall indicate throughout. How female beings in myth appear and behave can help all of us to probe into such questions as: What ways does the Feminine show itself in us, in our dreams, in our creativeness, in our troubledness, in our relationships, in our society? How can we enrich its ability to function and to help us? What deeper meanings can be ours if we relate to it through these mythic figures? What is the relationship between the Feminine and our psychological-religious task? And how is the latter related to divinity?

> To know the spirit of the Indians of the United States is to know another world. It is to pass beyond the Cartesian age, beyond the Christian age, beyond all the dichotomies we know, and into the age of wonder, the age of the dawn man. There all the dichotomies are melted away; joy requires sorrow, and sorrow joy; hard wisdom of experience joins in the rituals . . . the songs, the myths; idealism and ideality are joined with searching and undeviating practicality. And the child is joined with the man.

These moving words are from undated notes of John Collier, one of the great ones who sought to help and understand the Indian, and they stand true. I would only add, "And the Feminine is joined with the Masculine!" The rest of Collier's statement might have been written yesterday. It is as true now as it was then and as I hope it will continue to be.

Because virtually all the material presented from here forward will consist of mythic tales and their meanings as I see them, I will try to give a brief definition of myth (and include chants and songs) so that the ground on which I am proceeding will be defined. The older theories about myths held that they were tales told by primitive people, unlearned and superstitious to account for the universe which they experienced. This kind of explanation has been set aside. The contemporary idea is that myths are tales which have their origin within the human psyche, the same source which accounts for dreams and other unconscious manifestations. And the same source which gives rise to ancient rituals — societal and individual.

Millenia have passed since the first humans began to tell myths which, for them, described how their inner and their outer worlds were in relationship. In these primal tellings, probably, they believed this was how things were outside the universe. Today, with the insights of depth psychology — especially those of Jung — we know that myths are very faithful tellings of what goes on inside the human being. As one Jungian has written, "The history of myth is the account of the long struggle . . . of the slow and arduous work of internalizing that which had been externalized, of realizing on a spiritual plane that which had been naively lived out on the gross." (74, p. 9)

Contemporary medicine men and women in Indian tribes understand this depth meaning as well as the tribal meanings. The dreams of the people are also considered relative to the myths. Such things as "sings" and "chants" and "sand paintings" — all of which are used variously for individual healing — are based upon the myths. These myths are, in one way of speaking, tribal (or societal) "dreams." The various chantways that incorporate the myths are in a very real sense like the dreams and other inner experiences of an individual. And the chantways and myth tellings are, more often than not, precisely for the "healing" of a person who has asked for — and also paid for — treatment by the medicine man or woman.

It is important that this be understood as we move into the meanings of these great myths. The stories and the events in them are not for entertainment but for healing, for putting things in order. If we can listen to them and feel into them in this inner way — treat them as expressions of our own deeper psychological strata — they will speak to us in the same fashion, and bring us also a renewed sense of wholeness and healing.

Before moving to Chapter Two, it will add dimensions, I hope, to give two lists: (1) a comparison between Feminine divinities occurring in Pueblo and Navajo myths and Feminine divinities found in older mythologies, and (2) a listing of some of the attributes of Feminine and Masculine as I will be using the words hereafter. The attributes given are based largely on myths and mythic themes, art and artist's statements, dreams and other inner material from people in Jungian therapy. I have included space for the reader to add or to change the attributes chosen.

(1)

Major Navajo & Pueblo Feminine Mythic Figures	Comparable Figures from Other Ancient Cultures
More benevolent	*More benevolent*
First Woman	Prehistoric "Venus" cave figures, related to fertility.
Various "Earth" mothers, as Cornbeetle Girl or Mother of Corn	Cave as Mother. Mothers of Corn, Maize, Rice, fertility of crops and animals.
Lesser feminine animal helpers as Chipmunk Woman, Wren Woman, Bat Woman, Water Woman, etc.	Mother of Beasts, prehistoric & contemporary. Goddesses of animals, of the fold (Sumer, Babylon, Crete, Assyria, India, Egypt, Mycenae).
Spider Woman as helper, protector, spinner, as Spider Grandmother	Mother of "incubation" (Malta).
Salt Woman	Underworld of Xquic (Quiche Mayan).
More-of-everything-in-the Basket (Acoma)	
More malevolent	*More malevolent*
Changing-Bear-Maiden	Babylonian Tiamat as Chaos.
Snapping Vagina	Devourer, as Kali of India, or Le-Hev-Hev of New Hebrides.
Decoy Woman	Goddesses of Night, Death, Deadly Serpents (Greek Gorgon, Hecate, Medusa, Erinyes, Maenads).
First Woman (when shrewish)	Teutonic giantesses; Japanese Ugly Females of Yomi; Aztec Itzpapalotl, goddess of unpredictable fate; Bhavani the Destructive (throughout the Orient);
Spider Woman and Salt Woman (when angry)	Spiderweb as Maya, illusion.

Most revered

Changing Woman
(Whiteshell Woman and
Turquoise Woman)
Earth Woman
Corn Mother
Spider Grandmother
Hard Beings Woman

Most revered

Goddesses who manifest as
maids, mothers, high
queens, great powers for
good, either prior to or
more powerful than
male deities.
Isis of Egypt; Kuan Yin of
China;
Demeter and Persephone of
Greece;
Amaterasu of Japan; Bong
and Bomong, the light
bearers of E. India; Mary
as virgin and mother and
queen; Sophia as the
Wisdom figure in Gnosti-
cism; Aztec Tlazolteotl
who sweeps away
sinfulness.

In special relationship to the Masculine

First Woman/First Man
Wolf Chief's Wife/Wolf Chief
Snake Woman/Snake Man
Earth Mother/Sun Father
Thinking Woman (as both)
A 'wonawil'ona

In special relationship to the Masculine

Eve/Adam; Rangi/Papa of
Maori; Babylonian
Mummu/Apsu ; Nut/Geb of
Egypt; Izanami/Izanagi of
Japan; Shakti/Shiva of
India; (also perhaps all
Feminine beings whose
actions are usually in-
trinsically related to
Masculine beings, as in
husband-wife, mother-
son, brother-sister,
daughter-father, etc.)

(2)

DIMENSIONS
(PRINCIPLES, FACULTIES)

FEMININE	MASCULINE
(Attributes, Facets)	*(Attributes, Facets)*

creative changing, the capacity to flow, mutability "stirring up" (Jung)	creative unchanging the capacity to remain steady, immutability
uncreative changing, i.e., unpredictability or unsteady behavior	*uncreative unchanging, i.e, unmovability or fixedness*
operating in cyclic time (i.e., as moon goddesses)	operating in historical (linear) time (i.e., as sun gods)
movements inward, enfolding (like inhalation)	movements outward, thrusting (like exhalation)
mercifulness, compassion	justness, lawfulness
(negatively, as "mothering")	*(negatively, as "law and order")*
letting happen	making happen
substantially filled	
in myths, *usually* chthonic, earthy, or watery "creative confuser" (Jung)	formally exquisite
in myths, when destructive, usually by absorbing, swallowing, devouring or being substantially empty	in myths, *usually* heavenly, airy, or fiery *in myths, when destructive, usually by combat, weaponry, killing, or by being formally chaotic*

Feminine	Masculine
sensuously concerned with the esthetic attributes (colors, shapes, scents, tastes, sounds, touch, etc.)	rationally concerned with the ethical attributes (fairness, rightness, equality, truth, etc.)
initiates communion (as a bringing together) actions of relationship	initiates separation (as a making of distinctions between) actions of distancing
more inner-directed in general	more out-directed in general

(Readers may add here — with the reminder that
neither I nor you are describing male and female
gender but Feminine and Masculine in god beings
and in human beings.)

_____
_____
_____
_____
_____
_____
_____
_____
_____
_____
_____
_____
_____
_____
_____
_____
_____
_____
_____
_____

In my explorations of the Feminine, I am deeply indebted to the many friends, clients, teachers, and therapists who have been of inestimable help to me in understanding the Feminine in deity, in others, and in myself and my own dreams. Such helpers have been Dr. and Mrs. C.G. Jung, Dr. Gerhard Adler, Dr. Liliane Frey-Rohn, Dr. Marie-Louise Von Franz, Mrs. Linda Fierz-David, Miss Maud Oakes. There are so many other women and men in various situations who have illuminated my heart and mind by their own multidimensional struggles with the Feminine in their dreams and in their waking lives.

A particular gratitude goes to the former Museum of Navajo Ceremonial Art and its staff for much help over the years — especially to Dr. Bertha Dutton, the late Mary Wheelwright, and the late Fr. Berard Haile. (The former Museum of Navajo Ceremonial Art is now the Mary Wheelwright Museum.)

My methods of working the mythic material, the assumptions I make, and the conclusions I reach are my own, and I will stand with (or on) them.

For the reader, I hope that some growing edges of the Feminine will be encouraged and nourished in your individual soil to further the larger earth needs as well as your own.

For the Navajo and Pueblo peoples, may Changing Woman and Spider Grandmother — and all their sisters — preside over your lands, and help you to forgive that Masculine which has sorely hurt you, and recall the Feminine to the high spiritual place it deserves, for you and also for us.

II.

FROM THE FIRST

"There are no true creator gods for the Navajo," said Fr. Berard Haile to me shortly before his death. "There are only those deities who plan, and those who create from what is already there." What he was saying to me was that creation tellings are concerned with the givens of human nature, with the deep inner psychic movements of personality described as aspects of creation. That many Navajo medicine men and women healers know this — have known it for centuries — is made clear by a story I had from a friend some years ago. He was a psychotherapist, and he and two other therapists met with several Navajo medicine women and men to discuss aspects of psychological healing. There was, he told me, no problem of understanding one another because both Indian and non-Indian therapists understood dreams, dream symbols, and myths as symbolic statements of inner processes which could be understood as statements about psychological problems and how to work with them. They agreed amicably about meanings of myths and of myth (or dream) symbols, despite their cultural differences.

The myths of the Southwest Indians (as also myths of other groups) are rich tellings of how things begin — the great "as if" tellings of the inner movements of individual persons, and of individual persons banded together. And of each of us when new events are going on inside. This is what myths and dreams are — descriptions of various inner interactions and movements of creation in any of us. Myths are great dreams culturally tinted — but dreams that we can personally understand and that can help us to know ourselves more fully. As we examine these myths we need to open ourselves to them as we would to whispered messages of personal dreams and "hunches" and insights.

The Winnebago Indians talk of a particular presence in a holy rite as "our grandfather the sacred woman."* The Keres Pueblos have as their earliest named divinity Thinking Woman, sometimes female and sometimes male. In the Hopi people's creation myth, Hard Beings Woman had her dwelling from the very first of creation on the one bit of solid ground that existed. She "owned" earth and heaven, sky and

* From here forward all myth details — verbatim or paraphrased — will appear in bold face type so that any reader may work at mythic meanings before reading the author's.

sea, stones and shells and stars. She could assist and also destroy heroes on journeys. Tyler says of her (89, p. 84): "She is the mother of the Universe, standing co-equal with the Sun, and perhaps even more powerful. . ."

The Zuni divinity A'wonawil'ona is described by Stevenson (84, p. 23) in these words: "With the breath from his heart A'wonawil'ona created clouds and the great waters of the world. He-She is the blue vault of the firmament."

Another description of this rich inner aspect comes from Pueblo myth. Corn rites marking the celebration of life to come are being described:

> The third day is given to the Mystery of Mother Corn. It is Mother Corn who has conducted man from the nether world of his olden origins, up into the light of day and the life of this land. She has been his guide and guardian, food-giver and life-giver, and the source of wisdom and intelligence, and animals no less than men are under her protection, and, with cereal food, game also is her gift.
>
> The last dance is before the altar. The men stand with wands raised, emblems of the Mystery. But the dance is for the women, each of whom, at the last, receives from the Corn Priest an ear of seed-corn, for to their charge are committed the fields. The Song of Ending closes the rite.
>
> Early on the fourth day the camp is broken. But before the people depart an elderly woman . . . stands beside Grandmother Cedar and speaks. [In fact, she acted like a priest, giving to the people final words about their behavior, their need to be of one heart, and she lifted her hands and gave the final prayer to the Power Above for peace to all peoples.] (3, p. 30f).

First Woman

In most versions of the Navajo Emergence myth, First Woman and First Man are among the nine holy ones present in the first (lowest) world of darkness. First Woman (and First Man) are often described as coming from two primordial ears of corn.

First Woman is sometimes the deity in the east, co-leader and co-creator with First Man, and is put in charge of the first human beings. During the flood crisis of the Navajo (similar to other flood stories) First Woman listens to the needs of the people and tells them what to take along and where to go. Over and again First Woman listens, gives directions, advice, guidance. It is First Woman who receives the seed basket of Mother Earth for the first crops.

The Feminine as well as the Masculine is there in Navajo deities from the beginning. Thus both are inherent in all things. Present also are insects, and Coyote. This is a description of motion, process, first growths out of unconscious, unknown, and dark levels of instinctual being. As it is in early childhood. First Woman and First Man in some accounts were not only said to have been transformed from ears of lightning-struck corn, but were known as "our ancestors."

There is an insect called the Ripener by the Navajo. It is a symbol of female fertility, of life itself. While First Woman is not exactly the Ripener, she possesses similar powers of happiness and of life. In the Navajo healing myth/chant called *Windway* (97, p. 86f), First Woman is the one who gives birth to Earth, or to Woman-who-encircles-the-earth. Reichard says (76, p. 431) that Earth is either Changing Woman or is the mother of Changing Woman. Therefore, in one way or another, First Woman seems to be closely allied to, if not sometimes identical with, Earth Mother. Some of Her qualities as described by Reichard are very impressive. She is a creator. She made genitalia when humans came into being. She is a Holy One, and She controls witchcraft. She was the co-leader of the band of pre-human beings. She is difficult and very contrary sometimes. She also was the deity who cared for the greatest Feminine goddess, Changing Woman. The only known representation of Her shows Her in brown, the color of the Earth People.

Such beings as First Woman, Mother Corn, and Grandmother Cedar are figures representing our earliest creative awareness in its Feminine form. And this Feminine awareness is needed as part of our wholeness, whether we are men or women. In a later Navajo mythic world, when the men and women quarreled and separated, First Woman and some of the other holy people went with the men because the Feminine had to be present.

All of this is psychologically important because it indicates that the Feminine, reached even at this very early stage of consciousness, would be endangered if it split off from the Masculine totally. They belong together. If one or the other departed, the singleton would fall into the unconscious and would regress to a more primitive stage of development. First Woman and First Man together are the earliest "thereness," the givens, connections, "imprints" of the human beings, with Feminine/Masculine already present in the underearth world of beginnings. In this creation myth they are the two primal ears of sacred corn from which the earth is planted. And it is very important to remember that all created beings in Navajo myth are paired. From rain and snow to all birds and beasts to the humans, each thing has its Masculine and its Feminine aspects.

First Woman is a very early primal consciousness related to such things in our lives as our feelings, our person-to-person responses, our wants and desires, perhaps even our envies and hurts — and above all our choices of which ones to follow and which ones to avoid.

Very small children, under the stress of having to make a conscious choice, often avoid choosing by a thumb in the mouth or a cry for "mommy." Many an adult behaves much the same way — except adult sulks, or retreats, are slightly more sophisticated and rarely as endearing as the child's. If we could catch ourselves just before we are about to fall into such avoidances of choice, it could help us to call to First Woman in the hope that She might bring us a new consciousness.

A woman who was in therapy with me because she was desperately and too hectically trying to meet all the demands of a difficult husband, five children, and an active social life, dreamed that she was at a meeting, where all the noise and confusion irritated her. She tried to sleep but a vase of flowers near her was too small and kept spilling. So she went to look for a larger vase. Clearly here the dreamer needed to give better care to her inner Feminine side before any healing rest would be possible for her — inner or outer.

Further examples of ways in which this First Woman Feminine can become lost and suffering in any of us (and state itself inside us) are the following personal dreams (myths) and their meanings to the dreamers.

> I am returning from an ordeal of having been lost and believed dead. I am walking through deep mountain snow. During the way back my face seems to have been bruised into a different face — as if the old one is gone and I will not be recognized or remembered. A long time of cold, struggle, starvation. I see old friends in a village store but feel I cannot stop yet. I enter the home place strange, yet being seen as if I had not been lost or almost dead. I wonder why people I know can't see the condition I am in. Later on, as all my friends and family greet me as usual, I think to myself that what I have become is not apparent to them and cannot be shared. It seems it will always be clear in me and invisible to others.

This particular dream (personal myth) seems to speak for so many women who have gone through the deepest struggles and sufferings to come to a new recognition of themselves in their realities, and then are treated by others as if they were the same people who started out on the journey. In part, such nonrecognitions of change come because, on the whole, most of us do not want to face the fact that alteration of our person is either necessary or desirable. Moreover, we do not want to know that such changes, even if they are perhaps needful, entail suffering and struggle. The woman who dreamed the above took a long and suffering and struggling time working at precisely this return to her "old life" as a new being.

A younger woman, also working very hard to grow, and suffering with the changes, dreamed:

> A lot of girls are having a picnic. A group of older women are helping an even older lady across a very narrow bridge. She was virtually a 'basket case.' She fell from side to side while one woman, almost as old, tried to catch her and move her forward. I came up and took over, knowing that I felt love for the old lady and was able to help more than those who were trying.

This particular young woman wrote the following statement to me when she sent me the dream:

> I can recall two other similar dreams, one of a spider-like black heap of an old woman whom I helped into a car, and the other very important dream of a fat woman I knew needed love from me and I gave it knowing I would need to give more. This seems to be another version of the same lady. I feel, though, that here I am even speedier to size up the situation and move in. I'm quicker and more sure — an apt description of where I need to be. I need to be in constant contact with this old lady, knowing she was getting

older and more limp and therefore needing even more
strength from me. Of all the feminines thereabouts I
was *the* one needed and who could do the job. This
makes me feel more sure of my feminine strength and
wisdom. It also says, don't burden the old feminine
when it is my feminine ego of that very moment which
is needed. At the time, too, I felt it said to care and act
out of love and not out of expectation, not to care for
the old Mother part because I ought to but because I
loved that part.

She also enclosed this final dream for me to
read before our next meeting:

We were in a meeting. I was sitting by my therapist
and as we got up to go I sort of sat dazed. She got my
attention and winked at me understandingly and
said, "Come on," in a way that said it was O.K. I got up
and went with her. We stopped somewhere and I hung
back again. Then I took hold of her arm and cried. She
said, "Remember what we said as our motto before,
that other time, 'We must keep moving!' "

In each of these people — as their dream-
myths show — a deep healing of basic Feminine
separation-from-itself was needed. In each case
it was healing but not without pain and tears.
There is no other way.

In Navajo myth not only did First Woman
stay with a very demanding growth process until the suffering and struggle were done, but
then She created new holy things. She also
created male and female genitalia. She helped
to lift the sun into its place. First Woman (and
First Man) put forth much effort to help creation
and to guide the universe so that human beings

might avoid encountering uncontrollable forces. Humans must contact them by offering prayers, and usually they can be persuaded to help. Sometimes they cannot be persuaded. First Woman, according to Reichard (76, p. 77), "seems to be a rudimentary archetype of Changing Woman." She is often persuadable, and stands with the human beings as a prevision of the higher Feminine. We must never forget that She came from a primordial ear of corn, which gives Her the qualities of nourishing, earth, and fertility.

The excellent relationship between Sun and the Feminine is a part of Pueblo lore. Tyler (86) tells how the Acoma and the Sia Indians say the Sun is lifted to its place by a goddess or goddesses — and in some instances even seems to have been created by the Feminine deity.

In the final world of the Navajo Emergence myth, when Changing Woman is born, First Woman becomes the foster mother. Also, as owner of crystal fire First Woman is related to the ceremonial lighting of prayer sticks and tobacco. Her color brown is the color of the Earth.

Reichard has said that First Woman sometimes is seen as a class wholly evil and that, even then, She seems to have a "vision of a world made for (humans), and the purpose of bringing it into being. . . ." At the moment of emergence onto this present world, First Woman is the one who remembers what had been forgotten, because She says, "I have it next to my heart." (76, p. 5) It is She, also, who names the sacred building of the gods, the Everlasting Hogan. *

First Woman goes with the male opposite, First Man. She creates. She has potency. She has the word for naming things. Unsophisticated She may be. Unimportant She is not. She is holy, primordial, a seed transformed, a bearer of fire, creator of sexuality, lifter of the sun.

As fosterer of the life of Changing Woman, who is the greatest Navajo goddess, First Woman is the rememberer in her heart, — and yet, like the Maya and Kali aspect of the Hindu goddess, has the evils with Her also. This first branch of the tree of the archetypal Feminine in Navajo myth — how can we understand Her in relation to us?

---

* In Hindu thought the first appearance of energy, coming from opposites in motion, is shakti, the Feminine. Energy is something more than either opposite, is something new. As the Supreme Goddess (Bhagavati), the Resplendent One (Devi), it is the creative aspect of deity, the power which channels creation, which gives birth to gods. Danielou says: "Among the Saktas, who are worshippers of the Goddess, the source of existence, considered female, becomes the main representative of divinity. God is woman." Also She is Maya, Illusion, the chaos from which existence comes. She is "at the root of the three aspects of existence," which are, first, Reality, or "the power-of-coordination. . . of causation . . . of multiplicity"; second, Consciousness or "the power-of-understanding . . . of flow of knowledge"; and third, Experience or "power-of-delight . . . of destruction of world of illusion." She is the power of Shiva as Shakti, "a creative, all-pervading active aspect"; as Parvati, "a permanent, peaceful, all-persuasive, spatial aspect"; and as Kali, "a destructive, all-pervasive, time aspect." (20)

Living in a culture predominantly oriented toward the archetypal Masculine as well as to the personal Masculine aspects, it is hard for women (or men) to think of the divine as having a Her side. And yet that difficult phrase "Mother of God" still resonates in naves of cathedrals — some, at least.

In Greece, Artemis (Diana) was called Mother of the World, wearing Her many breasts proudly. Egyptians knew Isis as Mother of the Universe. How strange it is for many of us (except Jewish woman) to image the Feminine as the lighter of the sacred fire or as bearer of incredible challenges. Perhaps if we remember Joan of Orleans affirming her "voices" although it meant her death, or Jesus of Nazareth crying, "O Jerusalem, Jerusalem, how often I would have gathered you to me as a hen her chicks, but you would not!" we might understand. Neither the maid of Orleans nor the carpenter's son was deity, but each in a different way honored the Feminine power within.

What do we know of this primal Feminine sacredness in ourselves, whoever we are? Are we able to care passionately for ourselves, each other, our world, the inner Feminine? Can we "name" things, cherish them? Is it possible for us to speak of anything, even ourselves, as Rilke spoke of a gazelle:

> Enchanted one; how shall two chosen words achieve
> the harmony of the pure rhyme which in you like a
> signal comes and goes? (78)

This "signal" which "comes and goes" is the word of the simple Feminine divinity indwelling, is the creativity of First Woman. In its coming and going it is always there and always changing. In its purity it is eternal and "enchanted."

Let us look at a few examples of this archetypal Feminine as She appears in the dreams of contemporary people as a positive helper, even if sometimes in a strange form.

The following dream is from a professional man, married, but with occasional depressive moods which overtook him and sometimes rendered him almost powerless. During one such time he had this dream:

> A huge black bird wrapped a she-snake around my neck and tied her in a secure knot. It then put its claws between the snake and my neck and lifted me into space. We were in flight for some time and finally landed on a tall dark mountain which had no firmness, but seemed shadowy.

This is a strangely impersonal representation of that She Feminine who operates to help carry a person out of the darkness upward to a less dark place. The Masculine and Feminine act as one, but it is the Feminine who provides the means of lifting, who has the rope to reality imaginatively used.

During this same period of depression the young man dreamed:

> I am like a dark gray robot, painfully plodding along. Then a white dove appears with a white swan, bringing light and movement to my journey.

The dove was to him exceedingly Feminine, and the swan a mixture of Masculine and Feminine.

The dove seemed to him mostly the real helper.

The next dream is that of a woman in her early thirties who was caught in a tangle of being a mother, feeling rivalry with her married sister and insecurity about herself as a woman, and being also afraid to grow up:

> A small girl child came along towards me and moved and looked at me in a way that I knew she wanted to climb up to me. I took her in my arms as I would take an infant. But she was too old to be held that way.

The dreamer felt that this small girl was bigger than the dreamer herself had known, and needed to be seen as older than she had felt her inner child to be. Here the Feminine, both in the ego of the dreamer and in the unconscious of the dreamer, was working to make her more aware of her inner Feminine aspects.

A few weeks later the same woman dreamed:

> I am with a group at a lodge sort of place, of friendship and relatedness and God. At a meeting two older women, friends and teachers, were sitting next to each other and one was describing a new body awareness technique. They were sitting in rocking chairs and as the first finished her description she sort of rocked her chair onto the other's chair and they were close to each other happily rocking. Then the first one showed me the technique — and it involved sitting close together on the floor and winding in and out of the place of the other. It was good, and very mutual.

In this dream was the "pure rhyme," and the "enchanted," and the "signal" that "comes and goes" in the Rilke poem quoted earlier. It shows a part of the cyclically rich aspect of the She side of self and God.

First Woman, in any of us, is equivocal and somewhat disturbing. In the words of Reichard (76, p. 437), one of the great authorities on Navajo myths, First Man and First Woman seem over and over again to be in a bad temper regarding the humans. "They have an inkling of what is good and some desire to bring it about, but because of ignorance . . . they move back and forth between good and evil in a kind of experiment with the cosmos." This is what First Woman represents in any of us as we struggle and fumble our choices and our learnings, wanting what is good but over and over again frustrating ourselves. First Woman is related to the ear of corn and also to Sun and Moon and Earth.

For both the young man and the woman there was in these dreams, in differing manifestations, a caring and a passion and — yes — even an enchantment in the ways in which their inner parts were helping them to relate to the Feminine.

Three further dreams — all from women — serve to indicate how subtly the movements towards climbing up out of the unconscious condition occur, and also how subtly something in us tends to try to slow or stop the upward climb.

> I am on a submarine with many people, including an unknown male companion. We learn that very soon the submarine will stop functioning and we will all drown. Others did not know this. We start going down. The end is near. The man and I — each happily married — say that perhaps our spouses will meet and

come to love each other after this tragedy and marry. Then the submarine starts doing violent flips in the water, like a huge sea animal trying to save itself. Somehow it slides into harbor. We all slide off on long lines of kelp to the dock. I am amazed at how easily I slid.

A working girl has tethered her four-year-old boy child to a raft in a river while she is at work. Some of us swim out and tow the child and the raft to shore, telling the mother about a place that would care for her child.

I am on a ship and in a diving contest. I realize, as I enter the pool area, that it is a high dive and want to retreat but now I cannot. I am standing on the bridge as the ship pitches so that the prow nearly goes under. I move out and take the first dive. I return. I do a total of three dives. Each is in relationship to ship and sea so that my diving propels the ship into a different glide. The last dive is a swan dive leaving the ship running free.

For the first woman, in the midst of a real marital crisis that she did not really want to tackle as she knew she needed to, the dream showed her, first, that she was trying to avoid decision, and second, that the unconscious itself did not want her to give up and so it struggled mightily (as First Woman struggles in the myth to become) and in the end showed her that it was better to make the harbor than to drown.

For the second woman, well and happily married, with many children, the dream said her problem was her own work ethic and how it was endangering the life of her inner child. It also reminded her that she could do something else with that child's life.

For the third woman, working very hard to make peace with her mother and sister and to reconcile herself with a father problem and a divorced husband, the dream was showing her that, by risking her own actions with courage, her "journey ship" would be freer in its movements and thus would eventually take her freely where she needed to go.

Each of these dreams belonged to an "early" level of the growth process. That is, each was presenting the dreamer with possible ways of growth upward from mythic early stages of pre-human creation.

Moving a step beyond inner childhood and the earliest levels of creation, the next "world," developmentally speaking, is the difficult one of inner adolescence and, inevitably, of sexuality. Sexuality (genitalia created by First Woman) related to the Feminine aspects of selfhood is a sexuality related to the whole substance of beginnings and meanings. Sexuality related to the Masculine aspects of selfhood is more unidirectional, made up of urgent and thrusting desire. The archetypal Feminine learns, permits, shapes sexuality, while the archetypal Masculine moves directly into it. As givens, girls and boys alike have both Feminine and Masculine attributes. Neumann (63) refers to the "original hermaphroditic disposition" still being there in the child.

Recent work in genetics and embryology (at Johns Hopkins University, U.C.L.A., and Cornell University) indicates that for the first six weeks after conception every embryo is the same

unisex, Feminine. Scientists call this the "Eve
principle." Dr. John Money of Johns Hopkins
University was quoted as saying, "Nature's pro-
gram in differentiating the embryo is to form Eve
first, Adam second." (*Chicago Tribune*, summer,
1979)

Slowly Feminine attributes and Masculine attributes begin to take shape from genetic,
cultural, and archetypal forces so that, as we
grow visibly and invisibly, differences arise. The
Masculine attributes begin to be felt as "wrong"
for the girl, the Feminine attributes begin to be
felt as "wrong" for the boy. Nonetheless the girl
does have Masculine attributes as *inner* opposites to her more natural relationship to cyclic
time, and the boy has Feminine *inner* opposites
to his more natural relationship to linear time.

These are what the Chinese would call the
Yang principle in the girl and the Yin principle in
the boy. (Yang and Yin are also related to both
sexes.) Jung has given the inner opposites the
names of *animus* and *anima*, or the "contra-
sexual components" in each human being. (47,
48.) First Man and First Woman, at the beginning
of the Navajo creation, can be understood
therefore as belonging to each of us.

In our time, as part of the inevitable and
necessary revolt against the older and outworn
"puritan" ethic of repression, sexuality has
fallen too much under the domination of the
Masculine. Sexual encounters, doubled, tripled,
multiplied, are too often made into *the way* —
with too many of my own profession falling into
the trap of acting as if unconscious sexual

gratification equals relationship. Men and women alike today suffer from lack of real relationship, of what Tillich called "listening love" — although sexual encounters are free and pregnancy not necessary.

One man said to me recently, "No one loves anybody any more! People just grab for each other!" Or, as a woman in a contemporary novel says to a man who wants to "have" her: "Having's wrong, sharing's right. What more can you share than your whole self, your whole life, all the nights and all the days?" She refused him, telling him gently that she already knew the man she loved. (51)

First Woman as a deity representative of the elementary Feminine is able to move with sexuality as a shaping, as a genuine "knowing" of something to be later fulfilled in abundance. Her suffering in today's world must be intense when, as primordial Earth goddess, She is invaded and pushed aside with no concern for Her creative vessels — mountains, valleys, rivers, oceans. And it is little wonder that women are intensely protesting society's ways of dealing with rape — which all too often assumes the Feminine is evil and therefore is to blame for what happens to it. Archetypal Masculine and archetypal Feminine are two halves of a whole. When either one in any of its manifestations dominates or is dominated by the other, there is imbalance, unwholeness, unholiness.

In helping to raise the sun (as Isis of Egypt did also), First Woman serves our consciousness as it arises from the night of our dark beginnings.

She has qualities of both Virgin and Mother. As maker of the Everlasting Hogan She is continuity, enfolding life in a place and a space. She is, in each of us, the *taking time* to listen, to plant seeds, to acknowledge and deal with evil, to make plans for the future, which always begins now.

We do not take time enough for any of these matters, either in our personal lives or in our societies. Our evil we repress, deny, rename, or lay on someone else. Our seeds we fling out, heedless and indifferent as to whether they fall on cement, desert, or viable ground. What kind of beauty might come to us — in place of our denial and repression of our need — if we took to ourselves the following story of the origin of corn from the Zuni Origin Myth?

The Gods were proceeding upward from world to world during the Emergence. From time to time there was a rumbling of the earth and more new beings came out. Finally two witches emerged, a man and a woman. The gods rejected them at first, but the witches said, "We have things that are precious for your people." They showed the gods that their hands were filled with seeds. The gods said they would accept the witches. Then the witches demanded two children of the gods, a girl and a boy. Reluctantly these were given. The witches killed them and put them in the earth. Much time elapsed, and much traveling upward through many trials. Finally the ten Corn Maidens appeared from the earth giving the people corn — basic food made from these children. (81a, pp. 29-32)

In the psyche, this episode is a description of
how needful it is (1) to accept the unknown or unwanted darker sides of the Feminine/Masculine
in us — i.e., the "witches" — and (2) to be able to
sacrifice the youthful parts of ourselves in order
that more mature parts can grow into fruit-
fulness — i.e., Corn.

This is not easy to do. Youthfulness is
glorified in our western culture. I see in my
therapeutic practice and in my teaching so many
people who are miserably caught in trying to
look and act like twenty-year-olds when they are
in their late thirties or early forties. The outcome
is usually as sad as a handful of corn that has
never been planted, has never been allowed to
mature into true ripeness.

What can happen to any one of us if we
choose to move from a one-sided Masculine attempt to "keep things as they are" to a more
balanced approach to our lives by including the
Feminine in a conscious way? How can we do
this? First of all we need to recognize Corn
Maidens and First Woman as part of the larger
process of our growing into wholeness.

Here is a dream of a man who had worked
hard and aggressively to get ahead against great
odds and was nearing the end of his training. He
was married. There were children. The marriage
was beginning to improve as he worked at
himself. His entire orientation up to this point
had been male — physical strength, conquest,
revolutionary social views, drinking, fighting:

> I am in a foreign country. All the people are in some
> kind of special ritual dress. I am, too. We are walking

> through a forest in a procession. We come to a clear-
> ing. Suddenly I realize that there is a very high throne-
> like structure ahead, and one by one the people bow
> and pass on. When it is my turn I look up before I bow.
> There is a very huge ancient woman in robes seated
> on the throne. I feel fear and awe as I bow.

When I asked him what he thought the
dream was about, he said that he thought she
was the Old Wise Woman, or the Old Mother Goddess, and that he had to learn now what She really wanted from him. The dream made him feel
good, he said, although he didn't yet understand
why.

Another dream comes from a woman in her
later years, a woman who was a success in her
chosen work but who tended to drive herself too
hard:

> Seemed to spend much of a troubled night telling
> unknown others of the incredible work of the ancients
> in America in breeding and raising ears of corn.

She wrote the dream to me, being at that
time in another city, and she said about it: "It
happened by long, long, careful work of seed-
planting, tending, cross-pollenating, waiting,
reaping, etc. Always new deaths and rebirths,
new work for new corn. . . . This is . . . the process of conscious light-bringing, I guess." I
replied that I thought she was right.

And this dream, from a woman who had been
for many years very repressed and fearful of and
cut off from her instinctual side, is indeed what
happens when the corn is allowed to go into the
earth.

I am walking in a somewhat wild and wooded country-
side. I see a large leopard in a tree. He is light tan with
white spots. Then a large pure white fox comes up to
the leopard and speaks to him in cat language and
runs off into the woods. As he passed me he brushed
against me and I felt as if I had been brushed by the
gods. I could hear his words to the leopard. They were
something about Eeyore and then about Mercurius.

These were strange comrades indeed. Eeyore,
the sad donkey of the Pooh stories, and Mercurius, the quicksilver element from alchemy
—these two coming together in order to say to
the dreamer, gently and almost absurdly but not
absurdly, that the animal nature needed to be
heard and honored—this was a marvelous statement of letting seeds grow and produce as they
will, and of how, then, the inner "gods" come.

If we could open ourselves to First Woman
and Corn Maidens as part of "holy" beginnings
(of an hour, a day, a season, a life), we might be
able to accept and contain and alter our
unknowns rather than push them away so that
they poison us and our surroundings. We might
shape and honor our instincts, our substance,
our "earth" inside, finding them gracious comrades on the journey.

First Woman — in the opening scenes of
Navajo myth as in the beginning of our growths
from unconsciousness to consciousness — is the
slowly differentiating Feminine being. She is
maternal, persistent, substantial, firm, carrying
evils and seeds, concerned for the future of
humanness. She remembers all things. She is an
essential part of the sacred. When we have the
courage to remember what is and has been part

of our experience, and to accept it as "holy," this is the start of our singular destiny. First Woman then comes alive in us.

First Woman has many interesting and helpful dimensions for us as women. With First Man as her opposite, she began the process of creation. She (with him) is constantly transforming one substance into another. First Woman made the genitalia of the first human beings. She and First Man together were considered the first Holy Ones. She was the prevision of Changing Woman in the lower worlds. She mothered Changing Woman. Although she was difficult she was always needed. She is related to the very precious "crystal fire" which is used to light prayer sticks in Navajo ceremonies.

She is an essential and fallible Feminine part. She gets angry, commits unanticipated wrong behaviors, quarrels and argues, makes negative alliances with disreputable characters such as Coyote. Nonetheless, despite all these unattractive characteristics she is a Creator goddess, strong and forthright and willing to risk. She is, in us, a necessary courage which permits us to hold fast to the Feminine beginnings in ourselves, regardless of how awkward they may appear. She is the stubborn strength of the Earth in us, like a solid and honest peasant.

A woman who worked with me in therapy for a prolonged time was struggling to find her own identity, having had a bewitching mother who stole all her feminine courage from her. In the midst of some of the worst of the struggle she dreamed:

> I am lost in a vast building filled with impressive and smartly dressed women. I cannot find my way into the building. I am climbing up precarious outside stairs. I am growing more and more fearful. Just as I am about to panic and flee, a large rosy-cheeked peasant servant woman shows up on the stairs, reaches out a hand to me, and helps me into the building.

For her, the servant was in fact First Woman helping her to get into the ascent of creation.

Finally, let us look at the unfolding of a person in the thirties, struggling to let the Feminine live, a person who had tried in early years to please the parents by "putting on a show," by living up to all outside expectations. At the time of these dreams the dreamer was intensely working at getting free from the old Masculine-domination and at finding a newer and more whole way of being.

These dreams came within a two-week period:

> 1. I was in charge of our class show, but for some reason we hadn't put it on the year we were juniors (the usual), so now as seniors I had to do something about it. I was trying to schedule it, but I had to avoid this year's class show. I really didn't think anyone would want to be in it, but I was compelled by my accepted responsibility to try.

> 2. I went to a shop — jewelry — where my mother had gone. She was sitting at a table with a microscope looking at two things: the first was a key shaped pin, very small. When I looked at it through the microscope I saw that it was set with the tiniest of pearls, then a larger diamond and a red ruby. She told me it had been her mother's. The other object I don't remember, but it was more ordinary.

3.   I was on a ship and in my own room on it. I was thought to be sick or crazy, or something that put me in semi-isolation. Food was brought to me — soup — and when I spooned up the first of it, it had long blackish-gray "noodles" which turned out to be the tails of some black reptile-like things in the soup. (These feel reminiscent of the "baby alligators" in a previous dream which snapped at my heels to get me to look at the hurt.) I was nauseated and took my soup and complaints to the men in charge.

4.   My brother and I were having some dental work done. Some kind of tacks were put into our side teeth. Then we went away and were to return the next day. After school we both started up the hill and mother was also to go. I was walking and it was muddy. My brother came up on a horse. I wanted to ride the horse too. At the dentist's he had the two teeth with the tacks in them pulled, and I couldn't figure out why. Knowing they'd probably pull mine too I was scared and confused.

5.   There was a very tiny white house. There were three of us being directed by a woman to go out behind the house and perform a sort of rite by putting our hands in manure and sort of making gloves for our hands out of it. I think I was the only woman of the three. The woman director seemed like a woman but sometimes took on the face of my father. I was nauseated at the thought of this stuff. The other two did it fully, and just watching was very difficult. Then I had to do it — all the while hearing directions from the woman. I finally was able to put my hands flat in but couldn't make the gloves — only sort of a meatball roll. Then we went back around the house.

This sequence began to point the dreamer in a very new direction — moving her from a lengthy juvenile adaptation to a place much nearer to where First Woman and Corn Maidens could help her in a new beginning.

She began to see (Dream 1) that a "girlish" ethic was directing her to immature goals and immature responsibilities — neither of which were helpful to her. Dream 2, however, began to give her an intense and microscopically enlarged view of her Feminine heritage and its worth.

Then the psychic direction changed (Dream 3) into a true "descent" or "night sea journey" where loneliness and unpalatable substances had to be faced. Every truly creative change or creation or emergence has such times, when the heaving waters of the unconscious and the ancient reptilian food seem too much to bear. And the dreamer blamed the Masculine for not "doing things right" — while actually it was part of First Woman's leading her through the darkness upward.

She came then, in Dream 4, up against the desire to be like the Masculine (her brother), to ride the horse rather than to walk in the mud of the Feminine earth. And the "teeth of youth" must go to make a place for maturity.

Dream 5 was a good (even if distressing to the dreamer) statement of the absolute unavoidableness of facing the "messiness" of beginning to emerge from the darkness. Clearly the dreamer was witnessing the facts of darkness out of which all growth must come — from seeds to eggs to mammalian embryos. The little house was too white. The gloves of manure, in this dream, were saying to the dreamer that she could no longer hold life in hands that had not been clothed in darkness as well as light.

   In the words of an American poet, May Sarton, the need for First Woman is stated thus:

> *We think of all the women hunting for themselves,*
> *Turning and turning to each other with a driving*
> *Need to learn to understand, to live in charity,*
> *And above all to be used fully, to be giving*
> *From wholeness, wholeness back to love's deep charity.*
> *O, all the burning hearts of women unappeased*
> *Shine like great stars, like flowers of fire,*
> *As the sun goes and darkness opens all desire —*
> *And we are with a fierce compassion seized.*
> *How lost, how far from home, how parted from*
> *The earth, my sisters, O my sisters, we have come! . . .*
>
> *For we shall never find ourselves again*
> *Until we ask mens' greatness back from men,*
> *And we shall never find ourselves again*
> *Until we match mens' greatness with our own.*
> *(81, p. 77)*

These words — and this need — are as relevant
for men as for women, if our "greatness" is to be
found.

Salt Woman

Salt Woman, with First Woman, is among the very earliest holy ones in the lowest world. She plays a central and very influential role in the movements of creation. Before the destructive floods threaten the people prior to their final emergence on this earth, Salt Woman, walking in her usual solitude, discovers a baby floating in a whirlpool. She reports this to the other holy ones. (This same mysterious infant plays a crucial role in the stopping of the floods.)

When the people at last arrive on the earth, monsters populate it and everyone has to go into hiding. Salt Woman, First Woman, and First Man are the deities who survey the situation and decide what to do. On several occasions, Salt Woman provides salt that explodes and overcomes monsters who are threatening one or more of the divinities.

She also prepares broth for the twin hero sons of Changing Woman. At first it is too salty and then, when the boys grow used to it, it fortifies them against enemies. Thus her gift of salt helps the hero twins to overcome some of the monsters who attacked them.

In the *Shooting Chant* story, She is said to live at the center of the earth to be close to Her human children, spending winters on a male mountain, summers on a female mountain. The people must come to Her wearing special god costumes and singing Her song (or Changing Woman's song) in order to obtain salt.

In the final scenes of the creation story Salt Woman separates Herself from all other deities and goes on Her solitary way to a place of Her own — in most accounts a lonely salt lake.

In Pueblo myths there are also stories of a Salt Woman, a divinity who lives near Zuni and is married to Turquoise Male. She presides over and guards the salt for Her people. And when they come for salt, they make offerings of gratitude to Her.

Salt Woman is essentially introverted and quiet, related to water and earth, necessary for the life of the people, helpful if asked. She is also, in some uses of the word, "salty." She was "salty" for the twins — and "stinging" for monsters. She is austere, sometimes, harsh. She holds in Her possession that subtance which we find in all body tissues, in tears, sweat, blood; in the sea; a mysterious element not destructible in fire or in water; an element which can melt ice, preserve food, save life, even "grow" in a crystaline form.

It is virtually the final act in creation when Salt Woman goes to Her lonely dwelling beside the salt lake. After that, when people come for Her salt they must stand before Her and say,

"Grandmother, give me some water." The water
then will rise around the chanter — salt water —
and the need is met. In no other way can people
get salt.

How does She, as an early deity, differ from
First Woman? She is more solitary, more independent, more still. She sees things as they
are and relates to them as they are. Tears,
wisdom, savor, balance — She has these but
does not give them easily. She is not a wholly
nurturing aspect of the Feminine. She does not
demonstrate the attribute of enfolding.

If Her power is to be shared by humans She
must be sought out in Her isolation. Each person
must *choose* to go to Her, must know Her song,
must firmly request Her gift. First Woman is active, with Her seeds, Her tending and fostering
and giving advice, Her carrying of evil. Salt
Woman is remote, and changeless as salt is.

A very helpful way to grasp Her meaning is to
venture, with Jung, on a sidetrip into the field of
alchemy which "art" or "science" seems to have
been (and to be) "the herald of a still-conscious
drive for maximal integration . . . reserved for a
distant future." (43C) For Jung, alchemy was a
heretical field that spoke truths about the nature
of the psyche and the divinity which both
psychology and theology had denigrated or
failed to see. The processes of alchemy were not
the making of gold, Jung pointed out. That was
reserved for the so-called "puffers" (incompetent
alchemists). Rather, alchemy was the discovery
(or re-discovery) of the whole Self of individuals

by way of a hard work (*magnum opus*) of transformation.

This opus involved an arduous journey
through the darkness of the unconscious, a
death-rebirth journey not to be undertaken by
the timid, a journey which had at its conclusion
the *lapis philosophorum* or philosopher's stone.
Other names for this are the Self, the Atman, the
Diamond Body.

It is precisely this searching journey which
serves as the archetypal framework and content
of the majority of great myths, of the procedures
of analytical psychology, of our deeper attempts
to "find ourselves." It was stated succinctly by
the man Jesus: "Whoever seeks to gain his life
will lose it, but whoever loses his life will
preserve it." (Luke 17:33)

Salt is central as an alchemical symbol, central to the opus. In philosophical alchemy "salt is
a cosmic principle . . . [I]t is correlated with the
feminine, lunar side" of the alchemical opus as
well as "with the upper-light half." (45) It is
related to the unconscious in a central way
because it is the essence of sea water, that ancient symbol of the depths. Many alchemists put
Salt, Mercury, and Sulphur as a triadic formula
for the process — and in this connection Salt is
feminine, Mercury is hermaphroditic, and Sulphur is masculine.

Salt water, sea water, the crystal deposits of
salt — all these have deep symbolism in alchemy, and in dreams of modern people. "Whoever knows the salt knows the secret of the old
sages." For one of the great alchemists, salt constituted the physical center of the earth — as it

does in at least one variant of the Navajo myth. Salt is associated with whiteness and thus with a movement out of the dark of unconsciousness. It is also associated with bitterness — as in the Jewish Seder ritual, which includes the bitter herbs (herbs dipped in salt water) as a reminder of that suffering which is intrinsic to wholeness. Thus salt stands not only at the beginning of difficult ways but also at the end, to remind us of the unconscious as the container of good and evil, darkness and light, pain and joy. This miraculous salt or sea water is referred to in pagan as well as in Christian texts and has been used in rituals pagan and Christian. Salt also appears as *Sal Sapienta*, the salt of wisdom which, as Jung has pointed out, was better known outside than inside the church.

It is a difficult reach for our culture, so long dominated by the one-sided Masculine, to encompass Salt as Wisdom and as She and as invaluable. Little in our world helps us to seek out — indeed, to accept — this Feminine divine Wisdom, this Salt Woman, this deep inner understanding.

A dream from a woman in the midst of the struggle of letting her family grow their own way shows Salt Woman's qualities:

> It is time for me to meet the white witch. The meeting takes place at the base of a hill. She comes from a wood. She works with wisdom. She is older than ancient.

For this woman the dream was a joyful turning point in her growth. It helped her to pull away, gently and lovingly, from her family's demands. The white witch, the bottom of the hill, the wood — each spoke to her of what she called "nature's magic." And "older than ancient" told her of a deep well of salty wisdom that would not run dry.

For most of us, too frequently outer activity pushes inner movements aside as of less value, while Salt Woman waits alone beside Her woods or Her lake for us to desire Her gift and for us to be willing to pay the price for it. How can we go about getting in touch with Salt Woman? It needs a special kind of concentration, introversion, withdrawal from outwardness. We need to realize that life does have a savor hidden from us, but also that we can go more consciously into the unconscious and seek for it. This is a kind of prayer *of*, *from*, and *to* the Feminine. Such a "prayer" includes tears, sorrow, necessity, inwardness, stillness, understanding. And it is Her song to be sung to Her, not ours. So we encompass the salty harshness of the opposites of seeking and waiting. No salt of Wisdom comes to us unless we know our need and make the choice to take such steps as will bring us to the lonely lake.

Two other dream examples, both from one woman during a three month period of difficult psychological work, indicate how richly the contemporary psyche echoes the ancient ideas of "sea," "salt," "wisdom":

> Living in a big camp with many women and children. Went for a walk in fields beside the sea. Wrote two poems, one at the beginning of the walk, one at the end as a resolution of the first. I later told others that

this should always be done — a poem at the beginning and at the end of a journey — because "it is like
distilling alcohol from a large vat. It comes out pure
and clear." (Was aware of saying this sentence very
loudly.)

A few months later, after a time of hectic
outer work, she dreamed:

Deepest sense is that I was trying to escape people
and demands, trying to find times and places to be
alone, not spoken to. A feeling of vast sea coasts
where great waves pounded on a rocky shore.

And after two weeks of inward work:

I was living in, going on a journey in, a submarine. In
one room there was a bird in a cage, singing. Scenes
of seeing vast waterways from under the sea, of talking with a woman friend while washing the portholes
of my room and having a difficult time getting the salt
off them.

Distillation of the pure meanings by way of a
"work" (poems), the need to retreat to aloneness
for the finding of oneself, being under the water
with the singing bird spirit and the feminine
comrade to work with the salt — these details
show how the archetypal movement fits the
myth, or vice versa, or both. It is important to
point out that it is often more difficult for the
man to draw near Salt Woman than it is for the
woman. The cyclic nature of the somatic attributes of the Feminine are more known to the
woman — or *can* be more known. Unconsciously
the man can be swamped by the "sea," and in
alchemical terms he tends either to pull out of it

too quickly by way of "sulphuric volatility" or just to drown. The woman can drown, too, but she can also more quickly resist drowning by relating to rather than fleeing from Salt Woman.

Another and seemingly quite different facet of Salt Woman in the Navajo myths is related to certain positive witch attributes in the Feminine divinity. (First Woman has a bit of this witchness as the carrier of evil with the seeds, but on the whole She is more concerned with humankind's future, more maternal than Salt Woman.) Witchcraft is a major concern among the Navajo — as witnessed by the fact that one Haile version of the Emergence myth is told from the "evilway" or witchcraft side. (See 30a, also 60, esp. pp. 82-101, on witchcraft.)

Salt Woman has in Her power the mystery of an essence — salt — which is, as we have seen, both natural and supernatural. There is some truth in saying that perhaps the "witch" aspect of the Feminine is the "supernatural" manifestation of and control over the "natural" Feminine substance. Certainly a witch, male or female, is in all societies a person with magical powers which can be used for good or for evil. (For example, Merlin, Morgana le Fay, Gandalf, Saruman, to name a few from literature. And of course the witches in *Macbeth*.) In our time the word "witch" more often than not involves "evil." (However, consider also the word "bewitching.")

Among many primitive groups the "witch" and the "shaman" are not the same person. Perhaps this gives a clue to Salt Woman in Navajo myths, because Salt Woman is that combination of attributes of the Feminine which is shaman witch rather than negative witch. She possesses great archetypal powers, She forces people to come to Her in prescribed ritual ways, but She is not destructive, does not desire power over others, and gives of Her substance freely when properly approached.

Any one of us can, if we will, draw near to this Feminine shaman witch in our own psyche's depth and begin to understand healing. Children do this frequently, standing or sitting with a grave and solitary innocence in some still corner of time, looking at vistas we cannot see, singing wordless songs to that She shaman who gives Wisdom in exchange for their songs.

There are well-known mythic parallels to the withdrawal of Salt Woman. Amaterasu, in the Japanese creation story, retreats into her cave after her brother's misbehavior, and has to be tricked into returning. In Greek tales, Demeter withdraws after the abduction of Persephone. Egyptian myth tells of Tefnut's angry withdrawal into cathood. In most of these stories the goddess leaves because of some major negative act on the part of another, and in each instance is prevailed upon to return.

Salt Woman did not leave in anger. She chose Her solitude, to be broken whenever individuals came and offered Her song to Her in return for Her salt. Their coming was a matter of their own choice. Her motions of retreat and advance were not therefore seasonal or cyclic, but were determined by individual needs.

In her book *Singing for Power*, Underhill describes the incredible journey the Papago Indians took each year from the Arizona desert over the mountains to the Gulf of California to gather salt from the tidal flats of the Pacific Ocean. It was a four day journey each way, with very little rest or food. For the young men runners, it was magic. The salt they brought back to their people was related to the sea as feminine. The salt was called "the ocean's corn." The words of one of the prayer-songs give the feeling of Feminine power.

> *Now I am ready to go.*
> *The ocean wind from far off overtakes me.*
> *It bends down the tassels of the corn.*
> *The ocean water hurts my heart.*
> *Beautiful clouds bring rain upon our fields.*
>
> *(90, p. 132)*

What is the relationship between witch and this facet of the Feminine? Salt Woman could have become a negative witch if left alone forever with Her primal salt and no demands from humankind. Is it possible that some of our ecological evils are due to just such an ignoring of what Feminine Wisdom desires? Perhaps if we could recognize and acknowledge and ask for our portion of our meaning, our "seasoning," Salt Woman could become Sal Sapientia, very close to Sophia as divine Wisdom. When later on Salt Woman gave the Navajo hero twins salt to throw into the eyes of dangerous monsters, or when Salt Woman saw and reported the infant floating on the menacing flood waters, She helped to restore a balance. This removes Her from the company of evil or black witches and magicians who are never willing to sacrifice anything.

The Navajo idea (already mentioned) of
"evil" or "sin" as conditions where things are out
of order is completely in accord with what we
have just been exploring. Salt Woman, as well as
First Woman, is concerned with a restoration of
balance in the world. The Feminine in any of us,
women or men, as seen in these particular attributes called First Woman and Salt Woman, operates as that which can store or contain the substance until it is consciously and devotedly
asked for. Otherwise it will be loosed in chaotic
and unconscious ways to our harm. An example
of what must go on in order that we find the Salt
Woman part of ourselves and relate to Her
despite all the difficulties follows. This dream
came to a woman in her later years, a woman
who had been working hard and intensely for a
long time at her inner journey.

> I was with others on a long, long journey over a vast
> lonely terrain. There was a sense of long sweeping
> lands, with landscapes lonely and vast. Each person
> on this journey was to find his/her own leitmotiv or
> meaning. Once found, it had to be held, guarded, pro-
> tected. I seemed to be having to show others how to
> hold to theirs, to help them to do so. It needed
> courage, persistence, seriousness, much work. It was
> a mystery. I seemed to move from person to person,
> place to place, in slow and quiet motions.

The dreamer wrote to me: "I guess I have
been struggling this long day's journey into
night intensely for years. It is lonely, archetypal.
But it is also a unique journey to each one, each
with its own findings to be honored and cared
for. I must move toward it slowly and quietly."

This description of hers could also have been a description of the long journey to find Salt Woman. Each person's salt is unique, and takes courage, patience, and time to reach it. The salt so found must be kept and guarded and cared for. And this woman perceived her life at this moment in this way.

Creative men appear to have written more about this witch/shaman complementarity in themselves than women have. George Macdonald's novel, *Lilith*, and Rider-Haggard's novel, *She*, are characterizations of the negative witch aspect of the Feminine as seen by men, while Tolkien's Galadriel in *The Lord of the Rings*, and some of the feminine characters in the novels of C.S. Lewis and of Charles Williams, present more of the positive aspect, again as seen by men.

May Sarton, especially in certain poems such as "My Sisters, O My Sisters," and "Invocation to Kali," has portrayed vividly these two opposites as seen from the woman's eyes. The Bronte sisters made rich contributions which, although in some respects dated relative to cultural norms, communicate depths of the feminine barely touched by most contemporary "feminists." (32) In photography, painting, and writing, women are now able to present aspects of the Feminine almost impossible in earlier years.

What is important to us as persons in our world is that we know that we need and want the Feminine "salt" to preserve our lives, that we know where to go to find it, and that we know what rituals we must perform in order to have it. Stevenson gives a description of a trip to Zuni

Salt Lake and the Salt Woman who lives there. "After camping on the second evening it was with difficulty that the Indian was prevented from continuing his journey to the lake. The old guide said: 'You are Americans and can follow in the morning, but I am a Zuni, my Mother calls me, and I must go and sleep contentedly by her. Many years have passed since I have seen Her, and I cannot rest until I have reached my Mother.'" (84, p. 356ff) Stevenson goes on to say that the Pueblo people considered Salt Woman as a goddess, very central to them, very much a Mother Goddess, and worth working very hard to reach Her.

Inside the psyche it is the same. But we have almost forgotten how to turn toward that Salt Woman aspect of ourselves, that Salt of Wisdom. We do not know or will not sing, humbly and honestly, Her songs. We refuse to cross the inner mountains and deserts to the lonely lake of our unconscious realm. We flee from ourselves, we hide from our aloneness, we "keep busy." And She withdraws from our real being, drawing the curtains, waits, until we remember Her.

When we can come to Her, Salt Woman, as the eternal presence of deep and quiet and wise gifts, She then gives us our "savor" — the salty depths of our own sense of presence. This takes exploring, seeing, sensitivity, discovery, judgment, common sense, and the ability to bear solitude sometimes. Salt Woman, I believe, continues to wait for us to set our reluctant feet in Her direction.

III
INCOMPLETENESS

It is difficult to present Feminine characters from Pueblo myths, because by and large there are none with totally evil dimensions. There are witches in Hopi culture, witchcraft is feared even today, and both males and females can become witches. However witchcraft, Waters believes (92), is only a perversion of Hopi mysticism. Spider Grandmother of the Pueblo groups occasionally is menacing and difficult, but not negatively evil. The Hopi Kachina dances for "initiating" have the Feminine Kachina Whipper Mother, who carries whips to give to lesser whippers to try the courage of the children. And adults sometimes. But She is not really evil or negative in a deep sense.

The Navajo seem to be more forthright in their outlook. True to their philosophy, they see negativity and evil as manifestations of disorder — very real but also conquerable. So let us approach the negative aspects of Navajo goddesses with Navajo realism. Since it is so frequently the negative of any quality that we try hardest to avoid, the negative is one of the most important dimensions of the Feminine to be understood. It is only by *not* avoiding it that we can begin to grow into maturity.

With this in mind let us look into three separate healing chant stories of the Navajo; first, the *Endurance Chant* or *Upward-reachingway* (dealing with good power vs. evil power); second, a part of the story of *Where-The-Two-Came-To-Their-Father* (from the *Emergence* stories); and third, the episode of the separation of the sexes, also from the *Emergence*. All of these belong to the creation story.

Certainly the three female characters to be discussed — Changing-Bear-Maiden, Snapping-Vagina, and Wolf-Chief's-Wife — are very unlike in many ways. Yet in other ways they flow toward one another. Each one displays one or more negative attributes of the Feminine (including its weakness) and therefore each can serve as a model for ways needing change. Let us remind ourselves again, in this material especially, what was said before — that evil for the Navajo exists when things are out of order.

Most of the difficulties and anxieties that we face within ourselves can either be healed or accepted without venom if we can learn to handle dark things with the same love as light things. This assumes that we really know which is which — perhaps a dubious assumption.

But we do need to try to learn. We need to be as sure as we can that "the light that is in us not darkness," or that we are seeing our "beam" and not our fellow human's "mote," both intelligent warnings given by Jesus of Nazareth to friends and followers. We must also remember that deity and serpent are often related — as they were in Greek healing centers of Asklepion import, sacred serpents were fed as part of the cure.

Changing-Bear-Maiden
(HOLY GIRL)

The tale of Changing-Bear-Maiden comes from the myth of the *Endurance* Chant story as described by Reichard (76), Wyman (97), pp. 99-101), and Haile (30, p. 79f). It comes after the main creation and emergence events — but only just after — and presents some of the most negative attributes of the Feminine, including aspects of destructive witchcraft and sorcery.

A short time before the flood waters began to threaten the people as they emerged onto the final world, a young unmarried woman called Holy Girl gave birth "illegitimately, so they say," to a shapeless mass "like a gourd." For twelve days it grew, finally breaking open like an egg. Twin boys came out. The upward-moving people met in a council, saying that Holy Girl was not the mother, that the boys were in fact the children of dawn and evening. The twins grew up, never spoke, and one day disappeared, leaving only footprints. (In later mythic episodes they were said to be the brothers of, or bearers of, the sun and moon.) According to the Haile version (30, p. 79f), Changing-Bear-Maiden was first Holy Girl, then the Maiden-whose-clothes-rattle, and then Changing-Bear-Maiden.

In Wyman's version, used here, Changing-Bear-Maiden lived with her twelve brothers, all great hunters. She was very beautiful but she despised men. As a housekeeper for her brothers she was excellent, kept their home in wonderful condition, fed them and made clothes for them without effort. The brothers and sister were very content with this way of life.

However, one day Coyote came by the house. He stopped to talk. He said to her, "Why don't you marry?"

"I might," she replied, "but never to you!"

Coyote was very persistent and kept after her. Finally she told him she would marry him if he would die four times first. Reluctant to try this, Coyote brought his friend Badger to her house, when the brothers were away, and together they fetched wood and water to please her. This did not work. She still insisted that Coyote must die four times.

Coyote agreed. He cut off his genitals first and hid them, then he appeared to her as a skeleton. She beat him to death, stoned him to death, crushed him to death. At last Coyote reappeared to claim her. At this point she demanded that first he kill the great gray monster and bring the head home. Coyote did this, although not without employing considerable trickery, and at last she married him.

When her brothers returned from a long hunting trip they smelled Coyote urine in the house. So they built themselves a new hogan and moved away from the old one where Changing-Bear-Maiden and Coyote were living.

Reichard's telling of this part of the story is most colorful. Changing-Bear-Maiden, she wrote, exemplified

> . . . the Navajo model housekeeper and a member of an ideal family, for she did all the work for many brothers, apparently without effort. She kept their home in excellent order — cleanliness is particularly stressed — and saw to it that they had plenty to eat. The Brothers controlled rare game and were good providers; all seemed satisfied and happy with the arrangement.
>
> Into this situation, idyllic though in Navajo terms abnormal, came Coyote, overcome with lust for the girl and with jealousy of the brothers. He showed himself in his best light and made marriage seem attractive. The girl had been warned against danger in the abstract and had been taught a great deal of lore with which to protect herself, but no one had instructed her about 'the one man.' The description of the seduction of Changing-Bear-Maiden is a narrative gem. For days the girl met all Coyote's arguments and resisted his blandishments. She practiced all the theory she had been taught, requiring him to kill Big Monster and to undergo death four times at her own hands. Finally, she reached the end of her tests. Soft words and pity made her yield to him and she found out how 'nice it was to have a husband.'
>
> From the moment Coyote was allowed to crawl under the fringe of her robe she was in his power. During their sexual orgies he got control of her own and her brothers' secrets and she also learned something of Coyote's. The tale from here on recounts a conflict between the powers of the two, her recoil from the idealism of her virginal life, and the final conquest of both her own and Coyote's powers by the forces of good, represented primarily by Youngest Brother. (76, p. 414f)

One day, when her brothers were going out from their separate home on a hunting trip, Coyote forced himself on them as a hunting companion. During the hunt he bungled so badly that he was killed by Spider and Swallow People. The brothers returned and reported Coyote's death to their sister. Enraged by this news, blaming her brothers, she went on a killing spree. Her teeth gradually turned to bear's teeth.

In Reichard's words, "the horrible potentialities of the beautiful girl began to come out." She began to kill her brothers, one by one, and as each one was killed she became more like a fierce bear, until finally she was a monstrous, hairy, clawed beast. Before she could kill all of her brothers, the living ones managed to hide the youngest one in a deep covered pit.

When all had been killed but the hidden youngest — named Dwarf Boy or Spirit Wind — a messenger from the holy people came to Dwarf Boy's hiding place and told him that he could kill Changing-Bear-Maiden by watching her shadow and shooting an arrow into it at the right moment. In this way Dwarf Boy succeeded in destroying her.

He tossed her parts into the forest where they became good growing things such as yucca fruit, pinyon nuts, and chants. By using sacred lightnings and other rites Dwarf Boy brought all his brothers back to life and they became twelve holy people.

This Holy Girl aspect of Feminine being is virginal in a very negative sense. She walked away from, literally denied, the twin life born from the gourd-like mass. Any element of feeling seemed to be completely lacking.

(Her second name, Maiden-Whose-Clothes-Rattle, comes from the mythic tradition that she is thought to wear many sharp deer hooves on her clothes and hurts men with these hooves and thus possesses them — and the men are said to be under the influence of her ghostly (evil) aspect. Men possessed by her are in the grips of a negative feminine aspect — one of the many negative anima archetypes discussed by Jung.)

As sister of the brothers (for obvious reasons named Changing-Bear-Maiden) she is at first wholly caught up in serving the familiar Masculine expectations. In Reichard's word, she is the "model housekeeper" in an "ideal family." She acknowledges no mystery, prefers to ignore disorderly events such as birth, and tries to live as much as possible contained in the known routines.

Perfectionism without feeling gives a dubious security. Men as well as women can know a great deal about this aspect of harsh Feminine, although neither wishes to admit it. Every parent who puts the child's clean hands ahead of a warm heart is possessed by Changing-Bear-Maiden.

The perfectionist male — banker, doctor, lawyer, merchant, statesman, soldier, whatever — who places correctness ahead of human concern is dominated in part by this negative aspect of Feminine. Women in the professions can all too quickly be caught here. Disregard for what is being born — whether inside ourselves or in the outer world — can catch any of us in this negativity of a prolonged perfectionism that tries to remain in a precisionist Eden. And we have made a feelingless, faultless, cruel deity in this image.

To the extent that the Feminine is related to (not identical with) the unconscious — i.e., as in such symbols as womb, tomb, cave, forest, sea — when it denies living depths as Holy Girl denied the twins, and as Changing-Bear-Maiden traded lovingness for possessiveness, it is as if the unconscious was thereby denying itself and its own transpersonal needs. Unless this process is reversed our unconscious inner becomes destructive.

Perhaps this is related to negative witchcraft — as indicated when Changing-Bear-Maiden is described as having a "ghostly" way about her. In the history of witchcraft all witch covens, even into the twentieth century, when properly constituted are made up of thirteen people and the thirteenth person is the Master of the Witches, or the Devil. Changing-Bear-Maiden and Coyote each make a thirteenth when put with the twelve brothers.

Coyote is certainly in this tale (although not always) a sorcerer, related to the devilish, and uses his power for his own ends. Autonomous behavior, magical tricks, excesses, power plots, and manipulations, characterize him. Changing-Bear-Maiden also is a sorceress, power-driven, autonomous, plotting. Part of the Feminine takes on a devilish character and is thus demonically in league with an unpredictable part of the Masculine. The negative liaison of Coyote and Changing-Bear-Maiden is the reason behind her anger at Coyote's death.

Such angry negativity is manifested often by individuals in situations where part of the Feminine turns feelings (which might be constructive if taken inwardly and directed toward wholeness) into weapons against relationship; i.e., the anger that goes into cruelty to children and animals; the "cutting down" of one partner by the other through sarcasm; much that passes for "joking"; name-calling between two people or groups of people. In all such situations real relatedness is clubbed to death after death, feelings are seen negatively and reacted to accordingly.

In man-woman relationships or in friendships either or both people can, by denying and weakening the place of the Feminine, befoul situations by hostile and unreasonable demands (as Changing-Bear-Maiden's demands for Coyote to die four times). And in spilling personal poisons into the environment (as Coyote urinating everywhere) the Masculine dimension is misused.

Both Changing-Bear-Maiden and Coyote were essentially unwilling to work at problems, wanting to change things by magic and trickery and to remain irresponsible and insensitive. Coyote however, being bivalent as all trickster figures in myth are, survived and played a role in many other parts of the Emergence myth. Changing-Bear-Maiden grew more and more one-sided and univalent as she slowly became a hostile animal. Nothing could transform her except shattering.

Both men and women can be trapped in this "witch" complex of Masculine and Feminine negations. Often it is the man dominated by a strong mother who falls into the hands of his own inner negative "witch." He may be excellent in his work, fully able to carry responsibility in a profession. Yet with his wife, children, and friends his behavior is fussy; he carps about small things; he is stiff, critical, sometimes filled with self-pity or quarrelsomeness. He does not want to be responsible for his actions and his inner being. "Mother" should. She always was.

An example of his irresponsible unconsciousness, this refusal to examine what needs to be examined, is clear in the following dreams:

> 1) In my dream a man dreams that he has put into three cages a) a grey kitten, b) God, and c) a black widow spider.

> 2) My therapist and a friend are looking at my dreams, but I can't find the one just stated.

> 3) Another friend wants to photograph my symbols but they are buried in my knapsack.

> 4) I put a turtle in a cage.

At this time the dreamer was very resistant to all opening-up of the upheaval of the unconscious. Any examination of what had been hidden, buried, or repressed caused fear reactions with physical upsets. The negative Masculine was caging anything that might be unpredictable and thus upsetting. And the dreamer's Ego was burying anything that might be helping in new insights. Surely this is the negative Feminine that tries to devour (hide, forget, deny) anything that seems hard to handle.

Women who have been surrounded by brothers, or who have had weak, or negative and unfeeling, fathers, are more apt to be caught in a Changing-Bear-Maiden pattern. There is a deep, although sometimes not obvious, antagonism toward men. Such women tend to be perfectionist, overly independent, demanding of others, often irritable or angry. They also blame others for their troubles, and have a poor relationship — or none — to their inner world of unconscious depths.

Several dreams of a young married woman who was increasingly alienated from her husband show the problem of this negative feminine.

> I am in a store. I sit down beside R. He put his arm on my shoulder. I said, 'I don't want to be touched!' He made no move. I got angry and yelled at him, surprised at his persistence. I said, 'I don't want anything to touch me!' Some little animals started towards me — a squirrel, a cat perhaps — I didn't want them to touch me either.

> I am driving my car. My husband's ladylove was sitting beside me. I wanted to pull at her hair. I started pulling out hairpins. Then I realized that I was driving dangerously. I started pulling at her hair again, and almost crashed into an embankment.

> My husband came into the room where I was. He had some little narrow boxes. He said he had been out prospecting for poison. I wanted to hit him hard but I didn't dare.

These three dreams more than mirror the inner attitudes of the woman. Her hatred of her husband for his unfaithfulness was truly poisonous. She let live in her a fierce hatred of all life, almost — as the small animals she could not stand, as the dangerous driving, and as the desire to strike out violently. She was totally invaded by the angry and fierce Changing-Bear-Maiden Feminine.

If Changing-Bear-Maiden in the story could have worked at herself, could have related more creatively and feelingly to her brothers, she would not have been pulled down by Coyote's tricks. Because her "good" power was not dealt with responsibly, was poisoned by uncontrolled "innocence," she was caught and engulfed.

So with any of us. So with the people mentioned above. And so with our limitations of deity. If we let Her grow entrenched and defensive in a foolish Eden by making Her fit our negative Masculine images we ruin relationships, poison our surroundings, and are in some fashion "wiped out" before we can learn who She could be.

What brought about Changing-Bear-Maiden's end and the restoration of the wholeness (as twelve) at a new level? The smallest and youngest brother, the last one alive, the buried-under-the-earth Dwarf Boy. He brought about the transformation or rebirth. And this is an important fact.

The most insignificant member of the entire company, the last one to be thought of by Changing-Bear-Maiden — so lowly that She said, when hunting for him to kill him, "Where my excrement and urine fall, there my brother must be," — this Dwarf Boy was the one who restored the lost balance. He it was who could hear Spirit Wind. He it was who could overcome the negative Feminine by way of Her shadow.

Repeatedly, in dreams and in myth it is the lowliest which proves to be redemptive. The thumbling, the youngest, the littlest thing, the "smaller than small," is symbolic of the deepest Self, the Atman, the core of being. Why?

It is as if "majority rule" cannot make psychic wholeness. Because individuals are, as it seems, made up of many complementary opposites — Feminine/Masculine, Dark/Light, Water/Fire, Holy/Unholy, Child/Adult, — these complementarities need to achieve some kind of rapprochement in us. Unless each one of each pair has its place in the order of life, "disease" results. In other words, the inner archetypes and aspects of deity are not static but forever moving in us, inside us, (and in our outer world), seeking now this balance, now that.

And it is very often the "least" who is the makeweight precisely because the "least" is what is needed to move things in a different way from that of the "most." Something is hidden in the darkness — as Dwarf Boy was, as a seed is — so that new life can come when the situation is ready for change.

The well known parables about seeking for the lost sheep or the lost coin also point in the same direction. In such stories it is very clear that even the smallest, or lowliest, or least, must be included. To use Jungian terms, if our "shadow" darkness is not *consciously* recognized, it may be secretly known by our unconscious wisdom (Spirit Wind), and may then be passed on to the forgotten representative of our deep Self (Dwarf Boy), and hopefully this knowledge can lead, as in this myth, to renewal and transformation.

In the story of Changing-Bear-Maiden the balance between Feminine and Masculine — so basic in Navajo thought — is dangerously disturbed. (Things are evil, out of order.) Negative attributes of Feminine (see Table 2, Introduction) are in charge and also are in league with a Masculine trickster "sorcerer."

There is also a second way to see this myth as our own. We are shown a smug, "efficient," quite unconscious inner family —Changing-Bear-Maiden and her brothers. Status quo is maintained. No real feelings are tolerated. Hunting and household move in the usual ways.

Then an unpredictable, restless, questioning prodder enters — Coyote. He is the disturbing voice of the desert wanderer, and as an opposite to the well-organized brothers he is devilish. We tend to think Coyote is amusing when he shows himself in other people, but when he shows himself in us as an irrational purposiveness that unintentionally needles us by way of things we resist, he is not so funny.

Although we may try to repress or kill or set aside our emotional problems, we cannot do so when Coyote is around. We would like to rid ourselves of him (as Changing-Bear-Maiden tried to). Fortunately for us he hides his genitals — his reality is assured continuity whether we like it or not. Moreover, by Coyote's urinating in the house, the dark side is made unavoidable.

I could cite innumerable dreams of contemporary people about houses messy with urine, or feces, or dirty dishes and clothes, or uncared-for children — dreams which generally appear when the individual is trying to make everything "come out right" by ignoring many of the factors involved. The way the unconscious generally works at such a time is to bring the dirty and the smelly to the surface. By pushing the brothers to a new place the crisis of Coyote forced the entire situation to rearrange itself.

When we are taken over by a bad mood it works this way. We feel out of control. We "stink" — either by our own evaluation or that of a friend or colleague. If we run away as the brothers at first did, the situation catches us later. If we reluctantly let Coyote the dark one come with us, as the brothers eventually did, a difficult but important series of events is set in motion, which in the end results in a rather total transformation of all parts — Coyote, Bear Maiden, the 12 brothers.

The insignificant Dwarf Boy can see the "shadow" and redeem the situation. The negative Feminine aspect of deity is changed from harsh and dominating one-sidedness to a virtual cornucopia of growth — even though the evil must be dealt with in bits and pieces.

Western culture as a whole, and the majority of individuals in it, are deeply enmeshed in this difficult web described by the story of Changing-Bear-Maiden. Far too many aspects of Feminine and Masculine have been drawn into the prison of "efficiency" and "order." The creative Masculine has lost its thrust, the creative Feminine its all-inclusiveness. Much of our seeking — in psychology, in education, religion, politics, technology of all kinds — is done in well-kept and viewless places.

Let us return to the beginnings of this particular myth to that first sight of Holy Girl who did not keep her offspring. The "denial of maternity" theme does occur elsewhere in myth and folktale. There is an ancient Chinese tale of Notscha where the mother bears an amorphous mass and rejects it. Goethe's *Faust* has a series of "child disappearances" running through the entire drama — the most important being Gretchen's rejection of her child.

Perhaps one picture of the Faustian character of the West is that of individuals who do not reverence life and deity enough to accept them either in their poorest definition or in their finest. Somehow the casting away of inner psyhic "life" seems to lead to further denials. Holy Girl rejects the misshapen birth. This mass later becomes twin carriers of sun and moon after the first death occurs. Young-woman-whose-clothes-rattle becomes Changing-Bear-Maiden with all the deaths she demands.

In these mythic characteristics there is a marked and negative ambivalence toward that which is living. Yet perhaps this aspect of the Feminine is related not only to black magic but also to a death-rebirth cycle.*

* Isis and Hathor in Egyptian myth, Kali in Hindu myth, Hecate in Greek myth, Coatlicue in Mesoamerican myth, are each in one way or another partly negative, ambivalent,

(There is a fascinating ancient tale of an empress who is described as having many children but she insists on denying her motherhood until she can be reborn. She bears a daughter yet she is the daughter, remains a virgin, and is ridiculed by the people.)

Perhaps the Holy Girl in this sense remained a virgin despite Her bearing the strange "child." And She Herself was never reborn as Holy Girl. Her later regression into Changing-Bear-Maiden led to a kind of rebirth only when Dwarf Boy changed Her dismembered parts into various "living" things.

Jung has pointed out in more than one place that as long as the age of chivalry flourished in the Christian world the Feminine was more balanced and honored, with both its negative and positive. When chivalric attitudes faded the Feminine image became one-sided and was worshipped only as the unearthly and pure Virgin, not as part of the here and present earth. At this same period the great witchcults of Europe began. Murray (61), in her classic study of this phenomenon, feels that witches were carrying some of the qualities of the older pagan goddesses whose worship had "gone underground." In alchemy, too, the Feminine carried dual aspects and retained, as Spirit or Wisdom, dark and light dimensions.

and archaic deities. Most of these "witch" goddesses, however, are seen mythically as being many-faceted, as moving from negative to positive, as being both dark and light. Sometimes there is a split, and negative and positive are twinned in simultaneous manifestation.

Witches probably acted as helpful counter-poles to the Virgin in the Middle Ages, and might have kept a balance in the Feminine had the inquisition not made the situation schizophrenically cruel. That same pathological viewpoint toward the Feminine has tended in recent times to become planetary.

It is true, as Jung maintained, that one of the essentials of the Feminine is the acceptance and integration of suffering (*passus*, passion). Suffering has been inflicted on a global scale in this century, but Feminine acceptance and integration of this suffering has been, is still being, globally refused. We want security, safety, possession without pain, the right to do as we wish and to have what we want with the least output of effort. Thus we are, sooner than we realize, being brought face to face with specters of far greater suffering stemming from that cruel "possession" that inevitably follows refusal to suffer. Both men and women need to relate simultaneously to the Masculine gods of dragon slaying and the Feminine goddesses of suffering. Only in that way, with *whole* deities, may we be able to slay the true dragons and suffer the true suffering.

In our individual lives the negative and life-denying aspect of the Feminine, the Changing-Bear-Maiden in us, needs to be much more fully known. Where we choose *not* to choose suffering by doing such things as retreating from relationships, as *not* saying what our deepest feelings are, as *not* permitting ourselves to see realities — there where we have denied and backed away is precisely where we can become possessed.

Possessed by fear, possessed by self-doubt, possessed by darkness and meaninglessness —
these are the matters which invade us.

It is thus that the Negative Feminine can
draw us into false interpretations of events, into
illusion, and ultimately into horror. This is precisely what happened to Changing-Bear-Maiden.
Her other name, Maiden-Whose-Clothes-Rattle, is
very descriptive of what occurs when tenderness
and genuine caring are excised from our lives.
We are covered with icicles or knives or rocks.

The alternative is to choose to suffer the suffering of loving life, or listening love, or concern
for the world and other people. The nurturing
Feminine lives in and through such notions. Life
is permitted and nourished by them — as it is
when Youngest Brother (Dwarf Boy) of the Navajo myth is kept safe and therefore saves. It takes
courage to choose for reality because reality
always involves suffering of one kind or another.
The person who says, "But I can't tell her (him)
that! She (he) wouldn't love me any more!" fears
the pain of rejection so much that honesty is discarded and falsehood rots away the relationship.
Every child who is taught to tell the truth about
ideas and actions but not about emotions and
feelings is being taught one-sidedness and a
false security, is learning to deny the Feminine
by putting expedience before honesty.

On the other hand, even in the most devastating times of negativity it is possible to stop
and listen to Dwarf Boy and the sky doesn't fall
in! There is in us something small and buried
that can help us. Often when the negative "blowing off" runs down we can see, if we look, that in

the pit of the unknown, under all the stuff we have piled upon it, is a small aliveness and honesty which is transformative. It is safely hidden in the dark earth where our Changing-Bear-Maiden cannot get to it.

Actually in the myth it says that she can neither urinate nor defecate where Dwarf Boy is buried. No amount of dumping our wastes can destroy this valiant little being in us. And when Dwarf Boy is set free, this seemingly fragile Masculine element becomes the "smaller than small and greater than great," and is able to work with, to change, to alter the Feminine in its negative and uncaring aggressivity. The angry deity needs our Dwarf Boy to help Her become new.

Jung once said to me that "the shortest distance between two points is a detour," a statement which proves to be true in this tale. The long and harsh route from the perfectionism of the beginning, through the death-filled middle episodes, to the final transforming of Changing-Bear-Maiden into useful living things — such is the detour that leads from nothingness to aliveness, from negation to affirmation.

Swinging between opposites is never an end in itself. We need to be aware that there will be rises and falls both in our specific existence and in the evolving God-self-presence. We need to be able to recognize that we are in a mess, but also to know that we can understand it instead of eliminating it. We need the hidden and careful listening of love. We need to hear the small voice of Dwarf Boy and to act on his message. To the extent that we are unconscious, unformed, giving birth to things we disregard, getting caught in the outer appearances, we are in peril. The devastating shadow of ourselves is waiting to devour us.

A dream of a modern woman describes this state:

> I was in a sort of outdoor theater or meeting place. Another woman, a friend, was with me. Then a giant of a man, ugly, came toward us with a huge stone in his hand and meanness in his eyes. He was trying to hit my friend in the head. I was very afraid. Then a voice called, saying, 'Remember David and Goliath'! And I grabbed the giant's arm and stopped him.

This woman, one who always held her temper and kept everything cool, could not go on disregarding the brutal Masculine side of herself. To save her whole self she had to take the initiative against her own ugly giant in order to tip the scales in a positive direction.

If we work in our own patient way to be an "I," then we can perhaps learn that the suffering laid on us is part of the struggle of life itself and deity itself — is in fact part of the work of happiness. If we neither flee from nor identify with the Changing-Bear-Maiden part we can begin to find what to do next for, and with, Her. And the real meaning of Dwarf Boy and Spirit Wind is that we do have something "small" in us that can confront the destructive She and bring about change.

May Sarton says it for us:

Kali, be with us.
Violence, destruction, receive our homage.
Help us to bring darkness into the light,
To live out the pain, the anger,
Where it can be seen for what it is —
The balance-wheel for our vulnerable, aching love.
Put the wild hunger where it belongs,
Within the act of creation,
Crude power that forges a balance
Between hate and love. (81, p. 320)

Snapping Vagina

As a mythic character, Snapping Vagina does not have a lengthy tale connected with her. She is not mentioned in Reichard's two-volume work. (76) She appears late in Fr. Berard Haile's version of the *Emergence Myth*, shortly after the people have been created by Changing Woman. Here is how her making is described:

> . . . The Sun and Moon Carriers received dead personages as a payment for their journey made across the Sky, and out of their marrow mixed with Earth Grease by means of Sunlight was created the 'Snapping Vagina'. . . . Snapping Vagina and Smooth Rock (also a monster) bore the Kicks-off-the-Rocks Monster and Grey Yeitso (a threatening monster). They (Snapping Vagina and Smooth Rock) also mated with Big Star and produced Those-Who-Slay-With-Their-Eyes. Snapping Vagina mated with 'What-is-in-a-Mountain' and bore Tracking Bear and two Crushing Rocks; by mating with Milkweed she produced twelve Roaming Antelopes; by mating with a Reed she produced Cutting Reeds; by mating with a Rainbow she produced Moving-Sand-Wall; and by mating with a tree root she produced the Endless Snake.

> All these monsters now began to destroy the peo-
> ple and the Snapping Vagina went her evil way, com-
> mitting her adulteries, and was the wickedest thing
> ever seen. . . . (30, p. 63)

To hear this story as nearly as possible as it
was told to Fr. Haile in the cadences of Navajo
language is to feel a full impact of the negative
Feminine. Each of these various monsters issu-
ing from monster matings had its own particularized method of destroying victims. Snapping
Vagina's method was to sit down beside and engulf her victim.

When the Navajo hero twins, Monster Slayer
and Child-Born-of-Water, went forth from their
mother, Changing Woman, in search of their
father the Sun they had to pass through many
trials. Grown to maturity, and having succeeded
in passing their trials, they set out to destroy
the monsters that were harassing and killing
the people. The last but one of the monsters to
be dealt with was Snapping Vagina.

Monster Slayer — the more Masculine divinity of these male twins — undertook the task.
The Haile telling is vivid:

> He prepared red, blue, white and yellow stars and put
> one in his Red Flint. He then entered gray Mirage and
> sang a song to give himself power, and went to find
> the Vagina but was very much frightened when he
> saw Lightning shooting out of her body in every
> direction; this came from the opening and shutting
> of her Vagina. Monster Slayer sent his Red Star to cir-
> cle the Sky and she dashed after it, and he exhausted
> her by sending out blue, yellow and white stars,
> which she pursued. The Spirit Wind said, 'Attack her
> now; she is exhausted.' Monster Slayer touched her

with his Flint to see if she was asleep, and then put
his club in her open mouth. . . . Monster Slayer
then slew her with his stars and shattered her to
pieces, but she still whispered, 'Let there be a prayer
stick of mine for ceremonies,' and this is done today.

What are Snapping Vagina's basic origins
and how can we understand them? The marrow
of the dead mixed with Earth Grease by means of
Sunlight is the description. One fascinating
mythical connection here is that the bearers of
the dead across the sky are Sun and Moon carriers, those elements contained in the shapeless
mass born to Holy Girl and rejected by her. Perhaps the earlier indifference to the gourd-like
birth and the rejection of it by Holy Girl, and her
eventual transmutation into Changing-Bear-
Maiden, lead (in that indirect way of all myths) to
the monstrous Snapping Vagina and her ultimate fate.

Marrow is rich food, usually highly prized by
hunting peoples the world over. In this tale it
comes from the dead, from the lower world of
darkness and feared mystery. Earth Grease, pre-
sumably also a rich substance, comes from the
middle world of people. The means of mixing
these two rich substances — Sunlight — is the
brightest and hottest natural light humankind
knows about. It comes from the upper sky world.

Three levels of existence are thus repre-
sented — lower world, middle world, upper world.
Under certain circumstances this could be a
most auspicious combination making for wholeness. But this mixture seems *too* rich, much too
rich, too much of the core of death, too much of
the fatness of earth, too much of the cauldron of

light. It has a strange likeness to the explosion of an atom bomb, where the overwhelming light is a signature of overwhelming disaster. Shells, bullets, arrows, spears, come directly at their singular targets. Atomic explosions, like gigantic amoebae, engulf, "eat up," devour. Snapping Vagina seen in this way seems to resemble the maw of destruction which swallows up identity. She is the great devourer, whereas Changing-Bear-Maiden was the great negator.

The *vagina dentata* is well known in many myths other than Navajo. As an aspect of the Feminine She is intermingled with and at times almost identical with the archetypal Negative Devouring Mother. Snapping Vagina thus can be seen either as "negatively mothering" or as "destructive by absorbing or devouring." (Table 2, Introduction)

Hecate, Kali, Tiamut, the Medusa, the Gorgon, and all such Feminine deities spewing out their negativities are among the many manifestations of this archetypal Feminine. These goddesses and dragons, usually connected with death, are rarely gentle, usually hostile and angry devourers. (When gentle they are creative "tomb-wombs," containers to hold life until it can be reborn again in some fashion. Neolithic cave goddesses and many later goddesses of the dead were believed to hallow the dead, cradling them and preparing them for another existence.)

On the other hand, there are the Furies of Greek myth who call themselves "the children of Eternal Night," and who are described by a Pythian priestess as "a grisly band . . .

wingless, black." The ghost of Clytemnestra calls them "ye powers of hell," and Orestes says of them that they are "my mother's hell hounds."

If it seems difficult to encompass these negative aspects of Feminine goddesses we must remember also the manifoldness of the Masculine gods. They are seen not only as loving but as jealous, as cruel and punishing, as capricious, as judgmental, as besetting us behind and before, as one who forsakes us. (This is true even of Yahweh in passages in the Old Testament.) Such Masculine aspects of deity seem terrifyingly dark. Yet we learn and grow from them. It is much the same with the deity in Her negative Feminine manifestations. We can struggle with Her also — and learn, and grow, and thus alter the deity-human relation inner and outer.

Snapping Vagina is made from the elements of death and She is a devourer of life. She does not demand dramatic and bloody sacrifices as some goddesses do. She comes unobtrusively — else She could not sit down beside Her victims and overwhelm them. Where and how does She come into our lives? How can we know Her? And what can we do about Her?

It is a truism but nonetheless needs to be repeated that this She (with variations) is more often than not "discovered" in relationship to a mother problem of some sort. Women or men with mothers "who wore the pants in the family" (a male chauvinist image that is in this case helpful) often know much about Snapping Vagina.

If male, the individual may fear this She and find Her everywhere about him in the person of any female. But at the same time he may dream about devouring giantesses, which helps him (or would if he listened) to realize that a devourer lives *within* his psyche, eating up his confidence, eating up his creativity, smothering him in the cradle of his fears.

If the individual is female, she may take on the same devouring role toward herself at the psychic level, or toward others in her life enclosure — be they friends, partners, offspring, students, co-workers. She may identify unconsciously with an image of herself as only a womb to be filled, a thing to be satisfied. Never to love. There is little or no awareness of another. There is only a great void to be filled. The subtle and creative values of relationship are passed by. Such women manipulate and then snap up their victims like the "Venus flytrap" of the plant world.

There is also a major but hidden manifestation of Snapping Vagina in people whose egos are weak and hesitant. This leads them into feeling "eaten up" by others. Such people want to escape those others. The result is two-fold. The others are seen as Snapping Vaginas and are fled from. But they are fled from by way of addictions.

It is my observation over a long period of time that Snapping Vagina is operative in virtually all addictive behaviors — whether the addiction is to drugs, alcohol, tobacco, or compulsive sexuality. It is as if the individuals who are in flight from the outer demands just sit down and let the giant She of Snapping Vagina overcome them *from inside.*

In regard to man-woman relationships, there are very real differences in the way Snapping Vagina operates. If the man's Feminine side has been taken over by this She — perhaps lived out by his own mother — he is apt either to seek out a similar type of woman to partner his weakness, or he may shun all but the limpest of women lest he be again swallowed as in childhood. Often he succumbs to an inner "slut."

Such a man seems substanceless, almost shadowless, sometimes with an empty charm that is unconvincing. He may become impotent. He may grow misanthropic, snappish, a "confirmed bachelor" keeping his distance from all women even if partnered to one. Or, less often, his Negative Feminine takes over as a devourer, and he becomes like the Greek god Kronos who ate up his own children. And the children can be inner or outer, and get eaten all the same.

The woman whose mother has been such a Snapping Vagina devourer will either copy mother in her relationship patterns, or will try to be as different as possible from mother in response to others — men, women, or children.

For any of us, men or women, Snapping Vagina is true to Her mythic description. She sits down softly beside us and, before we realize She is there, suddenly we find that we are being taken over by compulsive behavior. Why is it so hard to control addictions? They are like monsters living inside us and ruling us, devouring us. We feel drawn inextricably to engulf every outer experience and to eat up every inner child, out of a deep, deadly hunger, a sense of negative emptiness. And there is no satisfaction for such hungers because there is no real responsibility being taken. There is only the terrible and continuous begetting of further monsters and more devourings. Emptiness, demand, unfulfill- ment, greater emptiness, snappish and exploita- tive demand, abysmal hollowness — so the end- less wheel of Snapping Vagina goes in our lives. It is a complete perversion of the organ of love, a distortion of Eros, a total absence of free giving.

But from this She, so much can be learned! In Her more active mien, with lightning flashing from Her in all directions, Snapping Vagina is awesomely terrifying. She fits very well into the negative image of deity — one of those explo- sively destructive deities who ruin fields, destroy ships at sea, prevent births, kill or kidnap babies. Often in this aspect of Feminine divinity She is, for the woman, "mouth-and-words" destruction directed outward. And for the man She is that which emasculates him from inside himself.

What does the Navajo account tell us about ways to deal with Her? First, it tells us that an in- ner principle (Monster Slayer) of positive Mascu- line consciousness — perhaps that aspect of de- ity which "separates" and "distances" (Table 2, Introduction) — must be recognized as *there* in us and as *helpful* to us. Monster Slayer is the more active and forceful of the hero twins. What he fully is cannot be answered until later when the deeper meaning of his (and his brother's) parentage is considered. Nonetheless it can be said that he is, as Masculine divinity, an aspect of courage tried in many fires and not found wanting. He is that part of the Masculine which undertakes creatively a journey to a center and which can then move from that center to deal with evil. Furthermore, *he does not destroy the evil She but transmutes Her.*

In most European folktales (and thus in the tradition we have known most about) "evil" is wholly wiped out. Probably this is so because these tales had their origins in a time when "evil" was more categorically defined and more repressed. Primitive myths — myths closer to people who were closer to the natural way of things — do not often do this because the "primitive" is better able to tolerate and encompass the ambivalences of life. What seems to be "evil" can sometimes be (and sometimes is) left in the hands of wisdom to work out.

In the Navajo chants connected with the healing rituals called *Red Antway* (92, p. 139f) there is a series of Thunder Prayers to be chanted during the healing rites for anyone rendered insensate by some kind of evil force. There are many repetitions of the phrase "the effects of the witchery of the evil thing," and of the phrase "the evil thing with its witchery." Then there are magnificent lines to the four Thunder People (Young Man Dark Thunder, Young Woman White Thunder, Young Man Blue Thunder, and Young Woman Yellow Thunder).

Here are some of the lines to Dark Thunder:

> *Whose home is of dark cloud, Young Man Dark Thunder, this day I have obtained your help, this day I have looked up to you for help, pleading with you I say*

this to you. Your shoes are dark flint, with these you will rise to protect me! Your legging, garment, hat is dark flint, with this you will rise to protect me!
Dark flints with four zigzag lightnings, which flash from you, with these you will rise to protect me! When you have gone with these to protect me, the monster will stop short of me there! The monster will miss me there, the monster did miss me there!

These same words are repeated to the other three Thunders, with necessary changes of color and semiprecious stones and kinds of lightnings.

In such prayers as these the things that caused the illness or out-of-orderness in the first place are used for healing in the hands of the helpful deities or demi-deities. So also in other mythic traditions. Athena, in *The Eumenides* (1), tells the Furies that they must not demand blood for blood, but on the other hand she tells the Athenian citizens that if they banish "the monarchy of Awe/ beyond the walls; untouched by fear divine/ No man doth justice, in the world of men."

It seems to be this way in the Navajo myth, in the episode of Monster Slayer and Snapping Vagina. The "evil" deity is, in one very real sense, not destroyed. As She was being shattered into pieces by Monster Slayer, Her last faint whisper was honored — "Let there be a prayerstick of mine for ceremonies." Her prayerstick is made and used in rites. The various parts of Her body became parts of the world of nature — as so often happens with Navajo monsters and giants.

So Her "evil" in this way became a medicine to help heal "evil." Nothing is totally destroyed.

A transformation ritual is used to alter the "devourer." The Snapping Vagina, the maw of uncreative possessiveness and thus of destructiveness, must be worn out. She must be taken inside the psyche by way of introversion and meditation. This aspect of negative Feminine has literally to be "shut up." Only then can the prayers to heal "the evil thing with its witchery" be chanted.

Often we must in fact *stop entirely* the overeating, drinking, smoking, rebelling, being promiscuous, demanding attention, sulking, etc., before we can learn what is behind our compulsiveness. Then the act which has become compulsive may at last contribute its genuine gift to our wholeness, whispering as Snapping Vagina did, "Let there be a prayerstick of mine for the ceremonies."

A woman who had come a good long way on her inner journey — but who, from time to time, was beset by a vast loneliness and darkness in which she felt separated from all people and things, dreamed:

> I am on a cosmic train — big, strange, impersonal, going across a cosmic land. I cannot find the room I am sharing with a friend. I cannot find the friend. Endless running through long corridors of the train, passing maids and other servants carrying trays. I am hopelessly lost, seeing nothing familiar and no familiar person. I go in mounting fear and a sense of impending madness and disorientation. I keep saying to myself, 'Where am I? Who am I? Where is anything?' I run up and down this cosmic train in rising hysteria. It was as if no one saw me, I was as nothing, as if I had been swallowed up by some enormous mouth.

This is a dramatic picture of Snapping Vagina. Because this particular woman was deeply aware of the things that went on inside her, she was able to work with this terror of being swallowed. She knew from past experience that she had to do exactly what was done in the myth. She had to call on Monster Slayer for help in reducing Snapping Vagina to a small size, or in changing the negative Her into something that could be handled. She knew, she told me, that both destructiveness and also the inner helper were part of her, and that it was up to her to tip the scales in the healing direction.

Another dream, from a much younger and very inexperienced woman, indicates what can be done in the earlier stages of such possession.

> I am holding the huge mouth of a lion or tiger wide open. The mouth is very large, like an alligator's mouth. It is taking all my strength to keep the mouth open, and the beast was getting angry. I knew that if I let go it would snap off my arms. I keep calling and waiting for help from someone who could put the beast to sleep or distract it long enough for me to escape. I am growing more and more tired and afraid of what I have done.

All this young woman could do at this point was to hang on. She did not know anything about the inner world, and she was deeply involved with two men, neither of them knowing about the other. Snapping Vagina was very much entangled in her life, and as yet she knew nothing about Monster Slayer. But her inner wisdom did know. It is to be hoped that she eventually understood it and followed it.

Sometimes Snapping Vagina appears in dreams as water, the sea, and so on. The following dreams are those of a woman, married, with children, and a loving husband, but with considerable unconsciousness in her meeting of life problems.

> I am at the edge of the sea, among many people. Many of them have staked out places on the beach and are digging for clams or oysters. The clams are too small to be taken, I realize. As I go further along the beach I see more and more black seaweed, and fear I will get tangled in it. The sea water becomes big waves, swirling like in a cosmic centrifuge. I am afraid for the children and others about. I climb up on the rocks. The sea has been sucked away, and I can see the bottom, with lots of the dark tangled seaweed covering it. I am afraid of it.

> I am underground, as if underwater. I have nothing on but a kimono. Then I go into another room underground. It is one of many, all of which are cut out of the rock. There is a shower, a big spray one, too hot. I walk past it and it follows me. I am afraid, and try to get out but all the doors have become windows. I call for help. No answers. There is a large closed eye on the wall. I put my finger on it, hoping a door will open. But my hand starts being absorbed into the wall under the eye. I waken myself in terror.

This woman had a difficult time handling the depths of the inner world. She learned how to deal with them later, with the help of her Monster Slayer masculine side. This He was her own growing consciousness of herself and of how easily in the past she had been swallowed.

By contrast it is interesting to see what happened to a young man in a similar situation. He was very intellectual, gifted, and almost entirely cut off from his sexuality and his Feminine aspects. Nonetheless he was gripped by mythic tellings and read much about them. Then he came into therapy, particularly to work out his sexual inhibitions. One of his earlier dreams was this:

> The sun had an awesome appearance. It sparkled ominously, like a giant Fourth of July sparkler. It seemed to be orbiting around the earth instead of the other way around. Its orbit was very close to earth. Within the atmosphere. It was relatively small compared to the real sun. As it whizzed by its orbit left trails of light, the way a sparkler does when twirled fast. It could stop whenever it wanted to. It seemed to have a mind of its own, almost an ethereal existence. It was powerful and frightening, God-like. Whenever it would go by I would hide. If it couldn't see me it couldn't hurt me. It was always there and when the orbit reached me I simply hid and accepted this horrible thing. I remember standing out in the open and watching this sun. It started going crazy. Its orbit no longer went entirely around the earth. It started going in circles right over my head and getting more and more frantic in its movements. It sparkled more brightly and seemed angry, as if it were going to explode. I was afraid but I kept watching it.

This could have been a completely terrifying dream of one aspect of Snapping Vagina and Monster Slayer. But the dreamer worked with it very courageously and took it head on — with the result that it was in fact worked out successfully. The "sun" did not go crazy. It was possible to resolve the sexual problems. And the negative Feminine was healthily transformed.

For each person thus far discussed, the way of "overcoming" the Snapping Vagina aspect was different. This is as it should be. Each individual has a particularized Snapping Vagina, and therefore the way in which Monster Slayer works is also different. The one element in common is the devouring aspect. Otherwise the "punishment" must "fit the crime." And what causes Snapping Vagina to operate one way for one person and another way for another person is no more and no less than what makes one person different from another.

Let me give two final examples. A middle-aged woman, professional, who had been struggling with inner meanings for her life for a long time, had this dream :

> I am with many people. One woman especially, a serving woman, is very vivid. She is possessed, half-insane. But I feel deeply about her, and sense that somehow we belong together. Then we are with naked people who are being put into oven-like places where they are heated in order to be healed of their psychic wounds, which seem to show as physical ones. They are healed, I see, although the scars from their wounds show. Somehow I and the serving woman together must go through this.

For the dreamer this was a deeply moving statement. To her, the serving woman was that part in her who was agitated much of the time, but was also often a gentler part. She knew that she had tried to "devour" those people whom she loved because of her deep childhood insecurity. She felt that in this dream the gift was to follow this "insane" side into the depths, into the inner heat, into the place of death in order to be transformed. She had to accept her inner "illness" and to take it along with her own ego-being so that both parts of her could begin to be healed.

The following dream belongs to a young man who was enmeshed in a net of self-accusation, self-rejection, and fear from a hypercritical father and a mother who clung to him.

> I am with a group of people, known and unknown. I suddenly hear myself accused by everyone — story after story of my behavior. I sat huddled on a couch. I wore a black suit next to my therapist. When I can't stand it any longer I get up and leave. People shout filth after me. I wait outside. When the group is done they all come out and condemn me. I cry out to my therapist. She comes, says we must get away from the crowd, and leads me to my car.

The dreamer here was seeing, within himself and in many outer situations, the Snapping Vagina as a castrating Feminine power against which he felt helpless — as he had before his father's attacks on him and before his mother's suffocating attitudes. To trust his therapist was to begin to fight back against the Devourer.

Thus the Snapping Vagina must be overcome differently by women and men — and yet this very ominous Feminine can be dealt with. We (women and men alike) are expected to brood the problem "inside the gray Mirage" as does Monster Slayer. If we do so, Snapping Vagina is transformed into useful growing things.

Wolf Chief's Wife

We return, in the story of Wolf Chief's Wife, to a longer mythic episode from the early part of the final world of creation. (There are more than 15 variants of this story recorded.) In this Blue World there were waters, sky, earth for growing, plants, animals. A supernatural and beautiful Round Hogan was built by First Man and his companions. In it were created male and female genitalia from jewels and semiprecious stones, and Coyote said: "These shall be birth." The people settled down and for seven years all went well with them. Children were born. Crops flourished.

One day, in the eighth year of their stay at this place, Wolf Chief (or a chief) came home to find his house in disorder, his children dirty, his wife absent. She finally arrived back, untidy, tired from play, indifferent to home. When the chief chided her, she told him, "Take care of the children. You have nothing to do except talk." Then she cried and said she was suffering. He found out she was having relations with another man.

In all versions a long period of difficulty en-
sued. In the Haile account, with which we are
chiefly concerned, the worried people sent a
transvestite (or Nadleh the Hermaphrodite) to
Wolf Chief, and finally the men decided to cross
the river without the women and start their own
community there. Nadleh went with the men
and brought seeds, cooking pots, and household equipment.

Both groups planted crops, but the men
used more rituals while the women were
careless. The men's farms increased more than
the women's. Both groups began committing
sexual excesses with themselves and with
animals, but the men had ceremonies to
cleanse their defilement.

After a long time some of the women tried
to swim to the men's side of the river and were
drowned. The next autumn the women pled to
be allowed to return to the men's side of the
river. After the women promised to keep peace,
they were returned on rafts and were purified in
ceremonies led by Marsh Wren Woman and Snow
Bird Woman.

It is particularly important in this myth to
take account of the mundane human incidents
because they afford us rich possibilities of
understanding our Feminine and Masculine at
the man-woman level, at the intrapsychic level,
and at the level of deity. The episodes and quarrels between Wolf Chief and his wife are recog-
nizable, poignant, and sometimes humorous examples of how men and women get entangled in

matters of relationship when nobody much is being conscious.

On a different basis we are helped to see more deeply into another aspect of the archetypal Feminine in its negative-positive expressions. The intra-psychic level will be considered first, for the very good reason that if two people were in the state that Wolf Chief and his wife appear to be, and came for help in straightening it out, the first step would be to see what was going on *inside* each one while each was blaming the partner for the problems.

Wolf Chief's Wife is of a different caliber than the two previous characters in this chapter. She is less thoroughly negative. Whereas Changing-Bear-Maiden was negative Feminine because of her aggressive denial of Feminine, and Snapping Vagina was a negative Feminine devourer, Wolf Chief's Wife is negative only in her initial uncreative changing, her rebellious unpredictability.

She is unconscious, emotional, upset, unhappy, in flight from any responsibility of relationship. But She obviously cares about the relationship, or She would not be so upset. (All this sounds remarkably similar to Yahweh's angers at His creations in parts of the Old Testament.) Through Wolf Chief's Wife the entire social body is divided. Masculine and Feminine beings are almost totally separated from one another.

Parted from the men by the Crossing Waters, the women defiantly take up a way of life doomed to fail under the circumstances. Rebellion without consciousness is futile.

Growth without opposites is eventually impossible. Systole-diastole of the heart, inhale-exhale of the lungs, action-rest of the body, night-day, seasons of earth, ascent-descent, the birth-death-rebirth cycle of all growing things: if one half completely dominates or tries to exist in isolation, disaster approaches.

In the story of Wolf Chief's Wife the Feminine dimension is not intrinsically negative. It is not *acting* negatively but *re-acting* negatively. This makes an entirely different psychological situation between two people, or within a single psyche, or within diety. Here the Feminine has been too taken for granted, has been "used" rather than related to. Quite rightly it is in a temper over this treatment. This is proper and can be creative.

However, when neither party — Feminine or Masculine — has the wits to deal honestly and openly with what seems to be wrong, there can be no widening of consciousness. They turn away from each other, angry and hurt.

Of primary importance for our explorations here, this part of the myth and its accompanying rituals give the best possible Navajo material on which to base a discussion of the complex and very often confused matters of sex, males, females, androgyny as a psychic state, the differences between sexuality and love, outer gender and inner bipolarity, (*animus* in women, *anima* in men), the relationships between Masculine and Feminine, and related psychological and spiritual matters.

A modern English writer has said: "So it is,

then, that the mystery of the spiritual conjunction of man and woman has taken to itself complete and autonomous self-existence as a living and visible portent in the night skies of the human mind." (88, p. 105) This "living and visible portent in the night skies" in deity, and in persons of either sex, has been a poor and misunderstood beacon all too often. Especially in our time. The conjunction of Feminine/Masculine has been misread, misused, and altogether abused for several centuries.

Jung, in his last great alchemical book, *Mysterium Conjunctionis*, followed with infinite patience, scholarship, and deep feeling the long and strange history of the alchemical ideas of the Masculine and Feminine, saying that for the great work (the *opus*) to be completed in any person, a genuine realization of and bringing together of the Feminine and Masculine opposites within the individual was essential (46). Alchemists talked in such images as "royal marriage," "heavenly nuptials," or "spiritual union."

The opus took place, as Jung has carefully pointed out, not in some chemist's laboratory but in the individual psyche itself (and perhaps in deity, or at least in the *imago dei*) — whether its owner was female or male in gender. Nor was this any easy task, this *opus*, as Jung also made very clear. In a letter written only a few years before his death (88, p. 11) he said: "The 'way' is not an upward going straight line . . . from Earth to Heaven or from matter to Spirit, but rather a circumambulatio of and an approximation to the Centrum. . . . We are not liberated by leaving something behind, but only by fulfilling our task as *mixta composita*, human beings between the opposites."*

Such a condition of estrangement can be seen contemporaneously within our larger culture and within the individuals of the culture. The Feminine attributes (i.e., "movements inward," "compassion," "bringing together," "actions of relationship") seem to be increasingly thwarted by the Masculine attributes ("outer-directedness," "making happen," "formal chaos," "destructive combats and weaponry").

In man-woman partnerships the split occurs if, when difficult situations arise and one or the other feels unjustly treated, the only answer to "Shape up!" is "Let me alone!" Then neither partner is dealing with an inner opposite or an outer one. Intra-psychically it is the same. If we are not honoring both the Feminine and the Masculine as they operate in us, if one of them (in this tale the Feminine) feels neglected and ignored, and if the only treatment is for the other (in this case the Masculine) to say to our inner feelings of need that we shouldn't have them and ought to snap out of them — this is the time we are likely to get drunk, go into a depression, quit our job, and so on.

A married woman in her thirties, struggling

*Wickes has a chapter titled "The Woman in Man" and another titled "The Man in Woman." In these chapters she defines lucidly and helpfully what Jung meant by "animus" and "anima." I refer the reader to this book and to other Jungian work rather than trying to elaborate further here. (32, 39, 43, 44, 46, 93) with family and husband and job, feeling increasingly frustrated and irritable with everything and everyone, had this dream:

> I am wandering around with a young man who is yelling "I am free! I am free!" He is in his early twenties. He is carrying a blanket. He is a 20-year-old baby.

This dream said to the woman that she needed to see that she was caught in the demands of an "adult baby" inside herself, a negative and childish Masculine that was poorly related to her real world. This Masculine baby in her was demanding freedom witlessly rather than looking at realities. Her positive Feminine was being shouted down by childish attitudes.

If the positive Feminine — that which can suffer, be distressed by suffering, have compassion, be all-inclusive, desire to enfold in an inward way — if this Feminine is being yelled at and harassed by infantile Masculine sides it is surely being robbed of its meaning. And its absence from the scene is a great loss. It was slowly recognized as a loss by this dreamer when she began to see that she must stop running away from the problems of her marriage and begin to try to resolve them.

A few further examples of Masculine/Feminine separation in the negative sense will make for greater clarity. This woman had a very difficult father problem — having had four "fathers" — and as a result her relationships with men were greatly distorted. One dream set forth certain aspects of this problem very clearly:

There is a celebration at the church, with soft lighting and young people doing ballet diving in the chapel to music. A school friend is there also. It is good to see her. Then I realize that my stepbrother is there drunk. And I see that my stepfather is in the same condition. I go to them and speak to them angrily. My stepfather grabs my arm and twists it, but I pull away and continue to say my feelings.

Here, surely, the Feminine and the Masculine parts of the dreamer show how alienated they had become because of the wounds from the very difficult family situation. Clearly the mother's problem was never solved, and this unsolvedness was then transmitted to the girl very early in her life. Her own struggles into adulthood were marred by this situation in which her mother spent her life. Part of the daughter's task, then, was the slow work of trying to reach a very different balance in herself, both through inner work and also outer relationships.

A quite opposite situation can also lead to a negative split between Masculine and Feminine. Another woman had been raised in a large family, with many sisters and brothers all very related. But she had never made peace with her own strong (and essentially creative) Masculine side. Here is a dream that came at a time when she was struggling to understand this separation:

A woman friend and I went to visit a man who made rugs. He could magically gather up materials and produce a very detailed pattern in seconds. I was envious of his power to make a rug this way. It was some sort of illusion, and he insisted that they would not last. He would not make us one to take home. When we

> brought out the rugs that we had bought they were all
> warped and twisted. We were horrified at what he had
> done.

She was still trying to manipulate life by some sort of "magic," to get things done as easily as possible. Her negative Masculine was living in her inner house and getting things "warped and twisted," while her Feminine side was not yet strong enough. It became so, with time and effort. And her creativity began to come into its own.

The following situation is entirely different because the dreamer was into her eighties when she had this dream:

> At a country place, walking in fields carrying a hoe. A
> young woman took my arm and asked me to go with
> her. We finally entered a building where people were
> gathered. She excused herself long enough to make
> an appointment for a therapy session, then returned
> and we went into a room where three women sat at
> small tables cracking almonds and hickory nuts.
> Across from them three men sat at small tables doing
> something scholarly. One of the men looked sick and
> unattractive.

This was indeed a surprising dream to the dreamer — but also a happy one. She had been working very hard at making peace within herself about her relationship to her dead husband and her relationship to her own Feminine. She felt this dream was saying to her, with a bit of a chuckle, "This is the kernel of the matter, and the women are saying so." And, two days later, she dreamed:

> I heard my own voice explaining to someone, almost in a whisper, "You know what young girls are!" There was pleading in my voice.

Here she had at last pled for the Feminine in herself. And not too long after that came this dream statement:

> I was living with my father and mother and one sister. I walked along the hall and was about to pass my sister who seemed to be a black girl. She leaned over and kissed my hand. And I kissed hers.

What a fullhearted acceptance of the Feminine came to her from this.

How very confused the Feminine can become in the woman's psyche is evidenced by the following dream:

> I am changing a baby girl's dress, but the top is too tight. I put diapers on, but she urinates at once, flooding herself and me with muddy water. I give her to another woman. Is she a twin? Then I am trying to get our house in order. My mother has given us all her old enema bags and douche bags and I don't know what to do with them.

This warm and feeling person, well related to her husband and children, was nonetheless handicapped by the inferiority and the confusion bred into her by her own mother's negative attitudes. She suffered from having been given stereotypical roles for the Feminine, and had to work very deeply with herself in order to break with them.

To return to the myth: With Wolf Chief's Wife

as instigator, the women in the myth behaved like the 20-year-old-baby in the first dream — making no attempt to look at realities or to find any way out of disorder except to proclaim their "freedom." Had the men in the myth acted as unconsciously, rushed as haphazardly into action as the women, creation would doubtless have had to start over.

There is in this myth, however, a rather unique healing element in the person of Nadleh the Hermaphrodite. Here is a true "media-tor," containing both Feminine and Masculine as a balance of values. (Nadleh refers to himself as one of the "women," yet is called "he" throughout the telling.) He represents objective feeling — conscious and detached from the quarrel but very present in all the movements of the people.

It is Nadleh who first comes to ask what is wrong. It is Nadleh who goes with the men, providing them with seeds, grinding stones, cooking pots. It is Nadleh who brings to the Masculine more wholeness and consciousness than the Feminine could bring at this point.

Nadleh makes it possible for the Masculine to utilize deep insights and rich ceremonies, whereas the Feminine goes away partial, unconcerned and unconscious. The men and Nadleh say, "Let us retire and see how our dreams will be," and they act accordingly. The women say, "Let them go. We can take care of ourselves," and then they proceed to waste their days.

This figure of the hermaphrodite is present in many cosmogonic stories. It is often connected with myths of birth and procreation. Among the Pueblo, Masau'u (Skeleton Man,

Death), is such a he-and-she god. It represents the integration of opposites in the god realm. It is the "divine" androgyne, the *complexio oppositorum* of alchemical theory.

Jung, in discussing the alchemist's concern with bringing opposites together — especially male and female — quotes a poem attributed to an alchemist of the Tenth Century. It is known as the "Epigram of the Hermaphrodite."

> When my pregnant mother bore me in her womb,
>   they said she asked the gods what she would bear.
> A boy, said Phoebus, a girl, said Mars, neither,
>   said Juno.
>   And when I was born, I was a hermaphrodite.
> Asked how I was to meet my end, the goddess replied:
>   By arms;
>   Mars: On the cross; Phoebus: By water. All were
>   right.
> A tree overshadowed the waters, I climbed it;
>   the sword I had with me slipped, and I with it.
> My foot caught in the branches, my head hung down
>   in the stream;
> And I — male, female, neither — suffered by
>   water, weapon, and cross. *(43, pp. 81-2)*

This poem touches many of the qualities of the figure of the divine hermaphrodite as it is found in the myths and rites of Egypt, India, Mexico and Central America, China, Greece, and in alchemical treatises.

The Hermaphrodite has been a worldwide mythic symbol of divine bi-unity — a quality of some of the oldest gods. The hermaphrodite is not in itself connected with the problem between the sexes but rather with aspects of the integrative process both within deity and within the individual woman. This theme occurs frequently in dreams and fantasies of people today — sometimes by way of known homosexual figures, or by male figures with breasts or female ones with a penis. The dreams can also transcend the human level and encompass larger levels.

The following dream belonged to a young man in the midst of establishing himself both in a profession and as husband and father, against a difficult background of poverty and a dominating matriarchy:

> I am with my analyst, walking outdoors. I said to her that I'd had a dream and in it the Godhead was an It, not a he-she or a she-he, and that the fact was troubling. She said, "But of course. The struggle with the he-she has only to do with the upsurge of the feminine and its concern for equality. The most ancient Godhead is an It."

The dream was far ahead of the dreamer, to be sure. It was a long and difficult way for him. But the dream helped him to begin to realize his inner Feminine and Masculine sides, and to see their relationship to larger meanings.

The presence of Nadleh with the men in the myth emphasizes the one-sidedness and unconsciousness of the Feminine here. With Nadleh present, the Masculine is aided by the Feminine in a very creative way, while the women have no counterpart to fill in their lacks. Thus the Feminine in this separated existence becomes more and more negative and useless. In the individual man this sort of negative Feminine shows itself in what Jung describes as "anima moods" — when the man is possessed by a kind of "inferior woman," childish, irresponsible, indifferently careless towards job, wife, family, commitments. Being "pulled down," "sulky," "living with a slut" — these are phrases men have used to describe to me how they felt when this negative feminine of Wolf Chief's Wife took them over.

In the woman it is as if her underearth and undersea forces of regression sweep away order, meaning, any real desire or capacity to work at life. "I feel as if I was groping around in moonlit darkness," one woman told me, "and I feel lost, but the worst of it is, I don't care."

The myth of Wolf Chief's Wife offers many insights. Certain actions are possible to us. If taken they can often reverse the processes of dis-ease and dis-integration. The wonder of mythic time is that over and over it takes us away from the profane into the sacred. This makes possible a new "in-the-beginning." Because of their relationship to Nadleh the hermaphrodite, the men have the gods with them and therefore the goods of the gods and the rites of the gods.

In the myth, the images of boats, holy people, sacred colors and jewels, hero gods, ritual plantings, are all images of "sacred" time. (This is the opposite of both clock time and wasted time.) The images are also paradigms for ways to restore the Feminine to a more whole place of balance with the Masculine in self and deity. Because the Masculine had all along included and honored the Feminine (Nadleh and other Holy People), the cycle of growth was not stopped. Even Masculine excesses were acknowledged and cleansed.

Although the negative Feminine of unconsciousness almost destroyed the community, the
Masculine plus the hermaphrodite Nadleh were
concerned with the well-being of all, with the
whole social organism. Nadleh and the company
of upper gods advised and assisted during the
long separation, and lent their presences to
cleansing and to restoring the Feminine to relationship again.

In a seminar for women where I used this
myth for discussion, I asked as a final question,
"After a separation of Feminine and Masculine
has happened to you, as it did in the myth, how
can you most help the re-uniting or healing process?" I asked that each person write out her
answer to this question.

Here are some of the replies:

I have to evoke Wolf Chief, to ask him to
return, to have the patience to learn what
made him go away. I guess I don't see what
he has to bring me sometimes.

The most important thing is that I see
now that this kind of thing goes on in me all
the time. Now that I've learned that both
sides are there I can let it go on until it's
resolved.

I need to open myself to the idea that it
may not come out right — that's the hardest.

I hope, when my onesidedness is skinny
enough, I can say, "Please."

When my energy is gone, has been eaten
up by the negative Feminine, then perhaps
the moment comes, the moment when I can
ask what offended me so much that I had to
get so split apart.

For these students of mine the archetypal actions and reactions in the myth were understood
at several levels. "Men" and "women" = Wolf
Chief and Wolf Chief's Wife = man and woman =
Masculine and Feminine in anyone = lawfulness
and steadiness, and compassion and mutability
= willingness to fight to live, and willingness to
suffer for others. These are only a few (not necessarily the best) complementarities and levels of
complementarity in my students' answers. Each
woman was struggling to get the opposites better related in both life and psyche.

The myth describes situations of dangerous
imbalance either within individuals or within a
society. Probably both. The positive qualities of
eros or *caritas* or substantial fullness have been
neglected. All-inclusiveness has been forgotten,
personal feelings denigrated, the deep well of the
unconscious polluted. *Logos* has become logic,
order has been legalized. Judgments are harsh
and the ego is inflated in the sense that "I" is
elevated above "We." The result is that the Feminine is swallowed up, engulfed by unconsciousness and resistance, and can no longer be a part
of the whole. The individual suffers from a psychological stroke, with one-half paralyzed.

Individuals (also societies and institutions)
are slow to recognize what has actually happened at such times. At first, feelings retreat and

ego believes itself quite justified in saying, "Let them go! I don't care! I can make it on my own!" Only with time, long time, "nine harvests" in the myth, does the full impact of the uncreativeness make itself fully felt. Only then is there a desire on the part of the Feminine to be reunited to the Masculine. The fault has been dual. Ego has become inflated on both sides, so cannot act as fulcrum between Masculine and Feminine sides.

A woman identified with aggressive and un-feeling *animus* (Masculine) actions, or a man caught in being rational, "objective," intellec-tually demanding — both are in places where the Feminine has been put into an inferior position and has, in its turn, retreated, gone uncon-scious. In each case life situations are met with "reasonableness" devoid of laughter and tears. Either we feel impotent to face the problem or we make ourselves not care. Hopefully these reac-tions do not work. Hopefully we recognize the need for re-union before it is too late.

It is also a fact that without the estrange-ment and anger and negativity nothing would have happened in the myth. It is only when we are able to express and face up to our negative feelings — about ourselves, about another, about our spiritual life — that there can be a renovation. All too often we cover up such responses, considering them "wrong." They only go underground then, confronting us from below with all the plagues of ulcers, divorces, corrup-tion in high places, hypocrisy, and their kindred.

Recently a young woman who had always shut away her angers and hurts (as a response to a totally unfeeling parental situation, among other things), told me in a therapy session that she had begun to find a way around this block. A man had verbally attacked her in a situation where she had been expressing her deepest feelings. At first she had tried to withdraw from her response. Then she was able to let the anger come up in her, and had dealt with it for the first time by painting and fantasying it out to its fullest extent — even to imagining putting a knife in the man's heart. The result was that she could return to herself and those feelings which had been almost cut off, and even to be somewhat open to the offending man.

Jung told of being asked by a Hindu whether it is the man who loves God or the man who hates God who needs the greater number of incarnations to solve his problem. The answer was the man who loves God, for the one who hates God is the one who thinks of God much more often. Jung went on to say that hatred is a great cement, that it is the one thing that often will break through unconsciousness to a higher level of awareness.

Jung also stated that, if someone came to him complaining of how difficult life is with those who are near and dear, that they are withdrawing, etc., he said to them:

> Of course it is most regrettable that you always get into trouble, but don't you see what you are doing? You love somebody, you identify with them, and of course you prevail against the object of your love and repress him, or her, by your very self-evident identity. You handle him as if he were yourself, and naturally there will be resistances. It is a violation of the individuality of that person, and it is a sin against your own

individuality. Those resistances arise from a most
useful and important instinct: you have resistances,
scenes, and disappointments so that you may
become finally conscious of yourself, and then hatred
is at an end. (101, pp. 4-5)

It seems, then, that the Feminine quality of
"letting happen" and the Masculine quality of
"making happen" come together through this
long separation in the myth. Nadleh the hermaphrodite, combining the best qualities of
Feminine and Masculine, is the instrument.
Nadleh is able both to initiate communion (bring
together) — a Feminine quality — and also to initiate separation (make distinct) — a Masculine
quality.

We must learn to recognize this Nadleh.
Nadleh comes whenever we can accept the sepa-
rations, the negative emotions, the loneli-
nesses, as things that can lead to reunion and rebirth at a more comprehensive level of being. If
we can learn to know — or at least to remember
— that there are parts of us that will inevitably
regress, be difficult, fall into bad moods, etc.,
then we learn that these very unwanted times are
precisely what will lead us to larger awareness
and richer living. One person said to me, "I guess
it is after I suffer that I can play, and after I play
that I can suffer."

This sort of self-knowledge comes with work,
with openness to the many parts within, with
permitting each part no matter how disagreeable
to have its feelings and desires. We must work at
and with the process, never forgetting the richness of ritual as we see it in the myth. Five
minutes a day will definitely not suffice to bring

the estranged Feminine and Masculine parts into relationship again. The bi-unity of the gods — of divinity — provides the reconciling element. Feminine unconsciousness and starvation, Feminine/Masculine dividedness, can be healed through calling upon and responding to the wondrous company of Nadleh and all the pantheon of gods of the Navajo.

What might it be like to be a person (or a society) that could be open to the help of such deities as these? If we can reach into the child's world of imaginative reality we may know. Or guess. If our psychological and spiritual rituals could be as new as these mythic ones, might healing be? How does wholeness come to be restored? There is no authoritarian solution. Resolution and restoration are based on response-to. The women spoke and acknowledged (responded-to) their own desperation and longing. The men responded-to their own longing and to the women's pleas. Nadleh and the other holy ones responded both to the Feminine and to the Masculine parts. The hope is renewal. The method is putting-in-order with feeling.

Photo by Margaret Burdge

IV.

TOWARDS WHOLENESS

There are certain mythic deities who are remarkable combinations of opposites although they remain in the Feminine domain. The Greek goddess Athena (in Aeschylus, though not in Homer) was a glorious mixture of mercy and objectivity. Kwan Yin in the Orient set aside her prerogative as one of the Immortals in order to take upon herself the sufferings of humans. Isis of Egypt was known not only as the wife of Osiris and mother of Horus, but also as Lady of Life, one of two serpents on the head of the Sun, and a goddess of dawn. Egyptian myth gives us Nut as well as Isis — Nut who supports the sky on her arched back. There are many others, lofty and lowly alike, who carry great Feminine strength and wisdom as well as tenderness and concern for "communion."

Innumerable series of creator gods, paired, are known throughout the world — in Polynesia, Egypt, Babylon, Mesoamerica, North America, Japan, as well as in Judaism and Gnosticism. In some cases the He-and-She is first a single creator and separates into two. In other cases they are two from the start, but equally acting in the creation.

One great heritage on the American continent as to culture, recorded history, and possible influences on North American groups, is Mesoamerican. The oldest and greatest god is a dual god, Ometeotl, of Nahuatl Mexico. Leon Portilla, one of the well known modern Mexican researchers into this ancient lore, described these twin aspects of Ometeotl:

1. Dual Lord and Lady.
2. Lord and Lady who nourish us.
3. Mother and Father of the gods, the Ancient God.
4. God of Fire, living at the navel of the earth.
5. Mirror of Day, and Mirror of Night.
6. Star which makes things shine, and luminous petticoat of stars.
7. Lord of waters, he of the solar brilliance of jade and of the petticoat of jade.
8. Our Mother and Our Father.
9. Ometeotl, who lives in Omeyocan, the Dual Place. (69, pp. 61-62)

Alexander describes these two principles at work together in a ritual of the Algonquin Indians of North America:

At the foundation of the world is the pillar of stone, the "Grandfather," the "Aged One," the abiding rock. Fifty paces before the entrance to the Medicine Lodge the pillar stands, fixed and unchanging through summer and winter, but now, for the festival, anointed and painted with red, the sign of life. With him must be associated the "Grandmother" of life, the living Cedar Tree, green the year long, but because she is symbol of the annually

fading and renewing vegetation of the earth and of
the unceasing drama of human passing and renewal,
each year she must be upreared anew, fifty paces
toward the sunrise from Grandfather Rock. The ritual
of the second day is the ritual of Grandmother Cedar.
(3)

He goes on to say that for nomads "the Sky-
Father, with his tribesmen the Stars, is patri-
archally supreme." But when humankind
becomes agricultural, when the human animal
changes from wandering and hunting and war to
producing food and goods, "there is a certain
feminization . . . and the goddesses come into
their own."

It is certainly possible (although not proven)
that almost before humans began to settle down,
when they were hunters and wanderers living in
caves, paleolithic cult objects had at least as
many Feminine as Masculine deity representatives. Womb-caves, fertility goddesses,
Mothers of beasts as well as of maize, rice, and
corn, have been found in many places as ancient
artifacts. It is almost as if the Shes, related to
underworlds and to heavenworlds, helped the
nomads to settle down. Who can say?

Alexander realized that "with the more
seasoned agricultural folk of the Pueblos the
whole ordination of living, their social cosmos, is
symbolized, or rather *lived*, in this dual mode, as
if the tribe were Man and Woman, like the
elemental human pair, the two-fold world, which
is also Man-Woman." (3, p. 81)

Among the Pueblo peoples there are several
divinities who are a combination of Masculine
and Feminine qualities. According to Tyler the

"ultimate Zuni god, A'wonawil'ona, is, like the Greek Phanes, a 'he-she.'" Such a statement can mean either that the god is beyond sex, or that the being contains the attributes of both males and females. (89, p. 81) Stevenson said of this divinity: "In the beginning A'wonawil'ona with the Sun Father and the Moon Mother existed above. . . . and below them were superhuman beings who labored not with hands but with hearts and minds." (84, p. 3)

There is also Hard Beings Woman, to whom belong the moon, the stars, and all hard substances such as stones, shells, and beads. She is "mother of the Universe, standing coequal with the Sun, and perhaps even more powerful." (88, p. 84) Thinking Woman, a creator goddess of the Keres Pueblo groups, belongs to the underworld but can think into space. She is sometimes male, sometimes female, sometimes both. The Hopi have a male fertility god who is known as "virgin of the earth." (82, p. 584) In the Pueblo of Sia, two Sisters (one more active than the other) are responsible for creating the Sun.

The greatest goddesses of the Pueblo seem to be, judging from the literature, Corn Mother (or Iyatiku), Spider Woman or Spider Grandmother, Thinking Woman (as already mentioned), and the two Sisters (best known in the Keres groups such as Acoma).

A Hopi leader (whose identity is not revealed by Courlander because of the nature of his study of Hopi myths) told the story of the early creation and the role of Spider Grandmother in this emergence. This Hopi telling is a true song.

> Spider Grandmother spoke to the people. Remember the sipapuni (emergence place) for you will not see it again. You will go on long migrations. You will build villages and abandon them for new migrations. . . . Tawa the Sun Spirit will watch over you. There are other gods as well.
>
> (Spirit of Death, Masauwu) — the spirit who germinates and makes things fertile . . . There is the Hard-Substances Woman who owns all shells, corals and metals. There is also Balolokong, the Great Water Serpent who controls the springs and brings rain. . . . The stars, the sun, the clouds and fires in the night will show you which directions to take. . . . If you reach a certain place and your corn does not grow, or if it grows and does not mature, you will know that you have gone too far. Return the way you came, build another village and begin again. In time you will find the land that is meant for you. But never forget that you came from the Lower World for a purpose. When you build your kivas (ritual places) place a small sipapuni there in the floor to remind you where you came from and what you are looking for. . . Only those who forget why they came to this world will lose their way. (17, pp. 39-40)

As we proceed to examine some of the Navajo material which parallels some of the Pueblo material, let us keep these Pueblo deities in mind. Above all, let us keep in mind the injunction to place a "small hole" (sipapuni) to remind us that all journeys are, eventually, emergences, and let us remember the challenging words, *"Only those who forget why they came to this world will lose their way."*

In a Navajo myth there are three major Feminine deities who will be considered in this final category of wholeness: Spider Woman, Changing

Woman, and Snake Woman. Each of them functions creatively in helpful and healing ways.

Each of the three — Spider Woman, Changing Woman, and Snake Woman — is quite different from each other. Their ways of functioning are unique. They are, however, each in Her own way, very ancient in the mythic histories. And they are wise. Spider Woman is earthy. Changing Woman is heavenly. Snake Woman is close to the human.

There are many minor goddesses in Navajo mythology — perhaps more than in most mythologies. As an example, in one list given by Reichard (76, pp. 596-97) of matched male and female beings in a chant there are 37 of each! Space does not permit discussing any of these at length, but naming some and a few of their attributes may add to the qualities of the Feminine deity's helpful power. There is Cornbeetle Girl, representing generative power in its feminine aspect. She is said to have given people voices. Bat Woman is in many of the myths as mentor, guide, helper, and is usually related to the east. Chipmunk Woman "has the particular power to aid in overcoming a cosmic monster" (76, p. 51), which makes her at such moments as important as the greatest of gods.

There is Cold Woman, necessary for keeping weather regulated; Meadowlark Woman who brings ashes to the enemy scalps in the war ceremony in order to make them harmless; Water Woman, who guides all small streams; Gopher Woman, a helper of the twin heroes; Water Spider's daughter, who heard and responded to Cloud when it was in need. In one variant episode from the text of a *Beautyway* sand painting, Lightning Woman takes a spirit boy, teaches

him medicine rites, and establishes female lightning
in the west. Earth Woman is often seen in sand paintings.

Probably most — if not all — of the positive aspects of the Feminine found in the minor goddesses is
to be seen in the major Navajo (and Pueblo) ones we
will now consider. Between them, or more properly in
the midst of them, Spider Woman, Changing Woman,
Snake Woman, and their Pueblo counterparts contain
the deepest and richest colors of Feminine being.
They are active, unique, creative, concerned, all-
inclusive. They learn, they teach, they assist, they
heal. We need each and all of them as representatives
of Her.

Spider Woman

Almost two thousand years ago in the San Juan Valley of the Southwestern part of the United States, a semi-nomadic seed-gathering people were already wandering and settling and wandering again. Whether thousands of years before that they came across the frozen Bering Straits, or whether some of them came northward from the Mesoamericas, there is not yet final definitive evidence.

The Hopis or Ancient Ones (Anasazi) settled into Black Mesa land. From wherever the Ancient Ones originally came, they probably brought Gogyeng Sowuhti (Spider Grandmother) with them and passed Her on to the imaginative Navajo as Spider Woman.

Grandmother Spider plays a central role in the Hopi creation myth. After the Sun Spirit had created the First (lower) World and put living creatures in it, He was not satisfied with what had been done, feeling that the creatures did not understand life's meaning. He called Grandmother Spider and asked Her to go to the creatures and get them ready to move on. She did so.

She led them on their ascent to the next world above. They improved for awhile, but then began fighting with each other and again Grandmother Spider was sent as the one to tell them and to lead them to the next higher world. Here they made villages and planted and lived together in peace. But the light was dim, the air cold. Spider Grandmother taught them how to weave and how to make pots, and for a long time they got on quite well.

Then dissension began. Again Grandmother Spider came and said they had to make some choices, and those who wished to change had to go further up. When with great difficulty they managed to get just below the "doorway in the sky," no one could see any way to get up there and through it.

At that moment Grandmother Spider and Her young warrior god grandsons appeared. Seeds were planted to grow high. Grandmother Spider urged the people to sing without stopping. This helped the bamboo sprout finally to reach up and through the "doorway in the sky." Grandmother Spider told the people that they must gather themselves and their belongings together, must ponder deeply what needed to be changed before they reached that doorway, and said She would return. "In the Upper World," She said, "You must learn to be true humans."

She and Her grandsons went first. During the period of the division into tribes and the settling into this new world, it was She who was always nearby, helping them to make what was needed, helping them to learn rites, telling them what was to be done to bring light and warmth into the world.

At last Grandmother Spider put a lake over the hole through which they had come and told them what they should anticipate on their journeys. Among the words She spoke were those quoted earlier, ending with "Only those who forget why they came to this world will lose their way."

> Grandmother Spider is all of womankind, Eve and Lilith in one, old to begin with wherever we meet her although she is capable of transforming herself into a young and beautiful woman when she wishes. Spider Woman lives alone, or with her grandsons between their adventures. Grandmother Spider directs men's thoughts and destinies through her kindness and wise advice, or lures to the underworld those whose thoughts and actions seem profane. (56)

In the creation story of the southeastern Cherokee (who are neither Pueblo nor Navajo), when the first people are struggling to create light and are not doing very well, a small voice speaks up from the grass, saying, "I am your Grandmother Spider. . . . Perhaps I was put into the world to bring light. Who knows?" She says She will try, and if something happens to Her it will not be like losing one of their warriors. She makes a tiny clay bowl, fastens some of her thread into it so She can find Her way back, and goes towards the sun where She takes a tiny bit of sun and puts it in Her bowl and returns to the people. The tiniest insight can be enough, the story seems to say.

The Tewa Pueblo tell of the usual journey upward from the deepest dark underground, with Mole as the digger. When the people emerge they are blinded by the light and want to go back. Then a small feminine voice speaks to them, telling them to be patient and to un-cover their eyes only very slowly. When at last they open their eyes they see the bent little old Spider Woman, grandmother of the Earth and of all life. She warns them about the temptations to quarrel and to have weapons and the sorrow that can come from them. She also tells them of corn and how to plant and tend it.

One tale of the Kiowa Indians tells about Spider Woman and a lost little boy who be-longed in part to the sun. He is found and taken in by a small ancient lady who lives alone in a tipi and tills her cornfields. Finally she lures him into her tipi — as his own mother was dead — and reassures him that she will care for him. When he asks her what he shall call her, she tells him, "You can call me Grandmother, for I am the Spider Woman, the mother and com-forter of all living things and beings."

The boy, through disobedience, manages to cut himself in two during the Grandmother's absence, thus becoming Twins, the famous Kiowa Half Boys. This led to the making of the Ten Grandmothers — rawhide cases represent-ing the overcoming of enemies of the Kiowa — and these bundles, named after Grandmother Spider, are still treasured today by the Kiowa.

For the Plains Indians Spider Woman is earth goddess. She is an "underground witch . . . friendly with her magic." (3) Among the Kachinas (sacred beings) of the Pueblo groups, Earth has three various appellations: "Mother of Germs or Seed, Old Woman, Spider Woman, Corn Maid and Goddess of Growth." (14, pp. 158, 187)

In many Pueblo groups Thinking Woman — who is often the supreme and primal creator — is equated with Grandmother Spider. (86) She is mixed — being creative, helpful, sometimes bumbling, very occasionally sinister. She is small, sits on shoulders to give advice, is wise. One contemporary Pueblo elder identified her as Keeper of the Fire.

The Pueblo are much more concerned than the Navajo with a certain harmony, to judge from those who have lived with and studied them and their thought. Tyler says, "What they most worship is a rough harmony in their universe. . . . They did not deny the existence of evil which has a supernatural force, nor did they objectify it to the point where their world was torn by factions of the gods. They were never the warrior children of any great god . . . [T]he first recourse was to various gods who might settle the problems in their own way . . . by a return to normal order." (88, pp. 259-60) Spider Grandmother is such a deity.

The Hopi myth of Spider Woman is different from most other tales of her. She is made by the male creator god in order that She may create life in the First World. The god says to Spider Woman, "You have been given the power to help us create this life. You have been given the knowledge, wisdom, and love to bless all beings you create. That is why you are here."

She did this, creating the hero twins, plants and animals, and finally male and female human beings. She helped the human beings up through the Second, Third, and Fourth worlds of creation.

In Pueblo myths She is also sometimes foolish and bumbling. Tyler says of Her: "Spider Grandmother is various. In contrast to the highest gods she is often at fault and her faults are the source of human bane. She had been creating perfect pairs, but a drowsy error led to the strife we experience today. What her mistake brought about was not the fall of man, but merely his unfortunate tendency to stumble over ordinary obstacles." (86, p. 96)

Spider Woman of Navajo myth is in some respects a close counterpart of Grandmother Spider of the Pueblos and Spider Woman of the Plains Indians. The Navajo carefully protect spiders, believing that Spider Woman is a friend and has to do with weaving, protecting the people from stinging insects, and teaching them things about corn planting.

In one version of the Emergence, Newcomb (67) relates that when the people were struggling to reach upward into the final world they could not quite make it. Then "Mrs. Spider, who had been hiding in a dark crevice, answered, 'If I were up at the opening I could spin a good strong rope from there down . . . but I have no wings and no way to climb upward.'" Dragon Fly carried Her up, She fastened a thread to him, then spun a thread down to the people. First Woman said to Spider Woman, "This is a very helpful thing you have done for all the people. . . . From now on you shall have a sheltered place in which to live, and will teach all who wish to learn how to spin strong threads and how to weave good rope and fine blankets, and you shall be known as the Spinner."

Spider Woman, the Spinner, the "little gray one who always lives in corners of houses," Grandmother Spider, Grandmother of the Earth, Thinking Woman — all these titles and more have been attached to this deity. She is a paradoxical "smaller than small and greater than great" — the *purusha* in the Feminine dimension. There is no single Navajo myth or chant which is Hers alone. She appears in many of the chantways and ceremonies, usually acting as a mentor and helper to struggling journeyers.

Sometimes She can be sharp, even dangerous — and even to the high gods — if people or gods do not treat Her with due respect. Her special elements are the spiderweb, down feathers, a never-emptying bowl, "unraveling strings" used in many healing chants, sometimes smoke.

In the Haile version of the Emergence, Spider Woman first appears in the Second or Red World and is not mentioned again until the time of the separation of the men and women (the myth of Wolf Chief's Wife). At this difficult time She enlarges Nadleh the hermaphrodite's house so that all the men can meet there and decide what to do.

Much later in the Emergence myth, when flood waters force the people up into the last world and monsters are after them, Spider Woman weaves colored webs to protect them until the danger passes. It is also told that She steals Water Monster's baby to further the Emergence.

At the beginning of the journey of the twin warrior gods — Monster Slayer and Child-Born-of-Water — Spider Woman is indispensable.

> They went on traveling and came to a valley where they met an old bent woman who asked four times whence they came; she told them that she had expected to see them, and asked them into her house. This was Spider Woman who had a tiny jet house, but by blowing on it she made it large enough, and brought them inside, where there were four rooms. She fed them by holding a White Shell where the light shone in it and filled it with Pollen; then she mixed water with it and gave this mush to them to eat. They were hungry and ate a great deal, but there was always plenty left, and the Spider Woman ate what remained in one swallow. She said to them, "Your father is very wicked and powerful, so take this living feather to help you later on." (30, p. 67)

This episode is typical of others in which Spider Woman befriends travelers and helps them to overcome dangers, especially in the impressive war ceremonial where She again rescues the twin warrior gods, feeds them regular food and then turquoise and whiteshell, gives the magic eagle feather, and steals from the Sun to help them. She also gives the twins the "life feathers." She gives formulae to quiet the anger of their enemies. She blows "flint and turquoise" images into Monster Slayer and Child-Born-of-Water to make them invincible.

In *Bead Chant* She helps the hero, Scavenger Boy, to overcome the monstrous Bees and Tumbleweeds. She spins webs to help the hero of *Flint Chant*. One impressive scene is that in which Spider Woman imprisons several of the high gods in a web because they rush through Her house without ceremony. She holds them there until they give her a ritual gift. Then She lets them go, giving them ritual sand paintings.

In *Windway* (96) She gives baskets at the place of Emergence. In the Hotchonji (Witchcraft) myth (30, p. 116f) She feeds the hero, who in turn kills the wasps that are eating Her Children. In the same chant, for the restoration to life of one who has been killed, She performs the final action of chewing roots and blowing them into the assembled body as veins.

It would seem that almost all of the positive Feminine attributes in the Introduction (Table 2) belong in some measure to Spider Woman. She tends to move inward, towards re-creation. Substance seems to fill Her. She is merciful and compassionate. The earth and all its cracks and crevices are Her rooms. She is concerned with textiles, threads, and with weaving loveliness. As is evident from most of the above episodes, She is concerned with "communion," bringing together, relationship. She is quietly inner-directed.

Spider Woman is not maternal either in the usual ways or in the negative aspect of "mothering." She is certainly not a devourer. Neither quarrelsome (though she stands up for Herself) nor submissive, in Her small house by the road or Her small web in the corner She works with the journeys of heroes and heroines. Her dwelling, whether web or the burrow of the desert trapdoor spider, is remarkable for strength, order, focus, balance, unobtrusiveness, security, skill.

As the spinner of the threads of fate or destiny She is sister to such beings as Norns, Fates, Graces. Eliade (25, p. 181) adds to Her dimensions in his discussion of the moon mystique. The moon, he says,

> has woven all destinies. Not for nothing is she envisaged in myth as an immense spider — an image you will find used by a great many peoples. . . . To weave . . . is also to create, to make something of one's own substance as the spider does in spinning its web. And the moon is the inexhaustible creator of all living forms. But, like everything woven, the lives thus created are fixed in a pattern; they have a destiny.

She is the Feminine as objective sustainer of life, with purpose and structure. Like a positive, concerned grandmother or aunt, perhaps. No nonsense about Her. Trustworthy.

Feminine objectivity — how we need that trait when tenseness, anxiety, and fiery affects get the better of us. We need to hear Her voice saying, "Now then, let's see what can be done."

There is also great containment and quietness in Her. Spider Woman does not hold-to. She very quietly opens-up-to. Softly but definitely she lets Her house be used when necessary. Usually

She opens to the Masculine dimension when it is endangered, giving safety, food from the never-emptying bowl, "life feathers," thread, webs, and always counsel.

Can we begin to imagine what it could be like in our lives if we listened for Her advice, let Her help us? We could learn, perhaps, that even the "god-like" Masculine parts of us are not permitted to rush about as if they owned the world. They must give as well as receive. We could also learn that there is this quiet place in us, like a deep cave of wisdom, which can be heard if we listen. We might discover this earthy light of substance as a part of deity in us which assumes that danger is also included in living and must be accepted rather than courted or fled from. When danger comes, something can be done if we slow down and proceed attentively.

Our inner Spider Woman does help if we let Her. She draws things towards a focussed center, and is symbolic of the purposiveness of life and communion. Among Native Americans She is very positive. Even the gods must stay related to Her.

Her meaning, as part of the indwelling deity in us, has to do with continual transformation, openness to that transformation, and a letting come the thread of destiny pulled from our deepest center. It is precisely this spider thread so gossamer fine that restores life to the dead parts.

How can we get in touch with our Spider Woman? How can this much-needed aspect of the Feminine become functional to men and women today? We seem to know less and less about letting life come from within our own substance. This does not mean "doing our own thing," doing just as we want and the devil take anyone who gets in the way. The "web of illusion" rather than Spider Woman's web seems to be around us and our planet, and our fate may or may not be already sealed.

Yet there is much we can do to work with our full meaning. Let us look once again at what journeyers in Navajo myths did to contact and be helped by Spider Woman. They listened carefully enough to hear Her small "sh-h-h-h" from the quiet grass. They looked carefully enough, standing very still, to see the almost invisible door to Her tiny house. They ate what She offered them and accepted Her feather gifts, Her admonitions, Her counsel. And they trusted and acted upon that counsel, giving Her gifts in return.

For so many of us the slow, the small, the hardly seen, the undramatic, the unflashy — whether in gods or in behavior — are considered of minimal value. Success depends on bigness, loudness, brillance, speed. Our current heroes and heroines are not, on the whole, quiet and retiring. One of the most often heard complaints by people new-come to psychological journeys is that things do not happen fast enough, or excitingly enough, or as well as Joe's work did when he went to that single weekend and had his life remade.

As an example of the hardly seen, the undramatic which is Spider Woman's way, the dream from a man who was afraid of human encounters shows how important the small is.

> There is a scene of a little boy crying. A man comes and says harshly, "Stop crying!" The boy keeps on. Then a small old woman comes and says, "Stand on your own feet." He stops crying.

The dreamer said that this funny old lady was the one that could help his scared child grow up. And he recalled how, as a small boy, he had always walked in his father's bootsteps in the snow. "I guess I've got to make my own steps, my size, not my father's," he said.

Another person, a woman, who was trying to resolve a difficult marriage crisis complicated by many petty details dreamed:

> I'm in an old cabin in the mountains. There is a big old spider web, and I get caught in it and fall flat. No one is there to help me. I try to get free. The spider scoots out the door. I try to step on it but I don't want to. I see my husband. I begin to laugh at my plight.

Here the little Spider Grandmother gave the perspective of humor so that the dreamer could proceed more lightly to deal with the relationship.

One of my most relevant examples of the work of Grandmother Spider at this point is taken from the material of a young man who worked with me in therapy some years ago. He was trying very hard to mature, to take responsibility for his life and his career since the death of his father. It was not easy for him because he was youthful and somewhat irresponsible and found play much better than work. And yet he was earnestly wanting to grow up. He dreamed:

> I am visiting a girl friend from many years ago. She is playing in the sand and water flowing through her living room, channeling it through a small landscape. I sit in part of this landscape with most of my clothes off. I tell her of my father's death. Soon I hear her singing a wailing song in the back bedroom. I go to the room and her guitar is lying on the bed and still vibrating by itself loudly. This continues until I ask her to play another song. She picks up the guitar and sings softly a song about flowers and I have the music in my hands.

Here the young woman was carrying the same role that Grandmother Spider often carries when She reminds heroes not to forget why they came into the world, or where they came from or what they seek. The young man was hearing the same sort of message from this singing guitar. The dream helped him to realize why — and how — he needed to grow up. How did it help? It told him, he said, that life goes on singing and we must have our music with us.

To be able to hear our indwelling Spider Woman deity involves many things. We must want to be on an inner journey. We must be willing to hear the small voice and follow its advice and eat its food. We must be generously grateful in giving such things as time, self-scrutiny, patience, and commitment in return for Her gifts. Graciousness at depth, unsentimental compassion, honest relatedness — all these are both given and asked for by Spider Woman and the Feminine values She stands for. We must get permission from Her to come into Her unassuming dwelling and receive Her food and Her blessing.

Children, I am convinced — and sometimes animals — have ways of relating to the values of Spider Woman. I recall sitting with a small nephew on a sofa while he fished with a string over the back. Once I spoke and he hushed me, finger to his lips. Magic was present. She — whoever She is — was watching us. My cat also had a way of peering endlessly into empty corners as if they held deep mysteries. Spider Woman could have been there.

How hard it is for us — who are neither small animals nor children — to gentle our adult selves enough to learn to sit quietly and watch ants work or tiny streams flow.

There are many dreams and life situations that fit some of the scenes of Spider Woman's activities. Two of them, one told by a youngish woman and the other by a youngish man, will give a good indication of what I mean.

The first has to do with a young woman who was working through a fiercely deprived childhood — not from a poverty of money but from a poverty of love. She had this dream in the midst of some of the most bleak times of struggle:

> Am in a city. Pass a home for orphaned or misfit children. I don't seem to see faces. Then I see a shockingly worse group of young things — limbless, growths like mushrooms and anthills where faces should be. Eyeless. A collection of life severely far removed from usual.

About eight months later she had this dream:

> I am called into a room for a surprise. There is in there
> a young child and her grandmother, a lovely old
> woman, with a gift of a small deer for me. I am filled
> with joy.

The limbless and eyeless blobs of children
are an infinite distance from the child, grandmother, and small deer. It was, for her, as if
somewhere Grandmother Spider had climbed into her life with all Her wonderful colored webs to
further the emergence of the dreamer.

Another example, very different, is from a
black American man in a life and death struggle
against the negatives of his life and his terribly
deprived background. One of his turning point
dreams was this:

> I am looking around in a place that seems unfamiliar
> and dark. It really is a familiar place, but somehow
> one that I am not wanting to see. I realize that it could
> be approached with eyes closed and ears unwilling to
> listen — yet a strong breeze pushed me past that pos-
> sibility. As I turned what I thought was a corner, I was
> met by a huge black eagle goddess. She was all over
> me — pecking and pecking and pecking! I thought I
> should be bloody but was not. I thought I should be
> fighting back but I did not. It lasted forever and when
> she was gone I was only aware of being thinner and
> my burdens much lighter.

This is a most amazing dream because of its
archetypal nature and yet its down-to-earth-
ness. The black eagle goddess behaves here as
Spider Grandmother often does — harrassing
and heckling and pushing "heroes" and
"heroines" into a better place than She found
them in. The dreamer wanted neither to look nor

to listen to where he was. And yet this Feminine deity forced him to do both. Without hurting him. And without his fighting back — which would have been his usual way to cope with things. He came out lighter of burdens. We cannot easily follow our dreams or our inner travels and elusive voices. We have forgotten how to watch the wondrous Spinner in Her quiet corners.

There were priestesses and priests at certain Greek healing centers who had to bid the seeker to come before the God. Spider Woman is not far from that place. We have to be bidden, to hear a call, and then we know that we seek life, or healing, or growth, or insight. Only if we know this can we hear Her voice.

(There are certain near counterparts in mythology who, though male in gender, possess some of Spider Woman's characteristics. All are related to healing and to helping humankind. They are personages like Chiron the centaur, Telesphoros the dwarf companion of Asklepios, Hephastus the smith, certain Teutonic elves and Celtic faerie. They are chthonic as well as helpful. But the difference between their Masculine dimension objectivity and Spider Woman's Feminine dimension objectivity is a difference in more active vs. more quiet, more thrusting vs. more patient, more fiery vs. more cool.)

Spider Woman is not easy to hear, either for a woman or for a man. The man is required to set aside his usual Masculine ego one-sidedness and to undertake a Feminine kind of sacrifice, risk, hardship. He must submit to the ego-deflating experiences of obeying small urgings, or going into little situations, of eating unimpressive psychic food, and of having, at the end, "only a feather."

The woman also must set aside the usual roles — whether they be job, career, service, family, doing for others — because the usual roles are ego roles and not the woman herself. It is perhaps (sometimes) easier for women than for men to hear Spider Woman, for the reason that women *can be* (not necessarily *are*) more related to nature's cyclic time by virtue of their own periodicity, physical and psychic.

In any case, in order to find this needful Spider Woman as part of a healing deity we must set an unfamiliar part of the psyche on an unfamiliar path. The hardest thing, perhaps, is the unimpressiveness of this Spider Woman way. The Feminine Spirit (wisdom, objectivity, purpose, continuity, delicate strength, the light of the matrix) is gravely needed by all dwellers on the earth.

Mostly we ignore the fact that in our Judeo-Christian culture Jesus the Jew brought the Feminine into central focus in his life and teachings — not as a one-sided "sweetness and light" but in all its robust and rich wholeness. Howes describes the "manifested feminine principle" as being symbolized in the early Synoptic books in three areas — the area of the meaningful Other; the area of the deepest inner attitudes of humans; the area of the rebirth-transformation process itself. (37)

An example of the first is the passage, "And wisdom is justified of all her children." (Lk. 7:35) An example of the second is the parable of the outcast Samaritan who alone cared for the wounded one, while respectable religious leaders passed unheeding. (Lk. 10:30-35) And an example of the third is the parable of the son who left home, was brought to a nadir of existence, took the long journey back (after he "came to himself") and was welcomed by his father's tears of joy at his rebirth. (Lk. 15:1-32) In each of these (as in many episodes parabolic, symbolic, and other) the Feminine has a vivid centrality for the process of renewal.

Perhaps the Feminine Spirit — accepting, outcast, gentle, hidden, and wise — may be able to draw the torn web of living relationship together again. Spider Woman is our mender of webs, our small helper on the journey of creation.

Changing Woman

Inasmuch as Changing Woman is primary to any consideration of the Feminine dimension in Navajo mythology and cosmogony, She must be included extensively. The summary of Her coming into the pantheon of gods — from the Haile Emergence — is this:

> After some period of time, a child was heard crying for four days. The people could not find the child. They were afraid. First Man finally succeeded in finding a mysterious baby girl. "[B]elow her stretched a Dawn Cord from the east and from the south a Sky Blue Cord, from the west a Twilight Cord and from the north a Cord of Turquoise. The child was rocking on Dawn and Turquoise Rainbows, supported by these cords." First Man recognized that Darkness was her mother and Dawn her father, and when he took her in his arms he found a small White Wind in her right and a small Dark Wind in her left ear, placed there by her parents. She was Changing Woman.
> . . . Initially she calls First Man and First Woman her parents, but the winds tell her this is not true, and even First Man recognizes she is not like other children. Soon she refuses their food and eats only the sacred Pollen. After twelve days she is full grown

and very wise, her periods begin, and a Puberty Ceremony is given for her, in which First Man is assisted
by Marsh Wren Woman and Bridled Titmouse Woman.
First Man offers both White Shell and Turquoise,
pressing them to the body of Changing Woman "who
thereby was made part of the fun."
Finally Changing Woman quarrels with First Man,
First Woman, and the others from the lowest world,
saying, "You are not my parents. Others took care of
me. You had nothing to do with me." She separates
herself from them, setting up her own dwelling in the
west similar to the Sun's house in the east, guarded
well, rich with the sacred stones. Her twins are born
after she is well established in this place. She helps
in the making of Man. (30)

She is definitely the favored figure among
the Navajo Holy People. Even Talking God, in
most ways the highest of the Masculine god-
beings, in *BlessingWay* calls himself "Changing Woman's child." Wyman called Her "the
most beloved deity." (98, p. 348)

Changing Woman seems close to the Greek
Athena, both in Her strength and solitude as
goddess, and also in Her apparent relationship
to parthenogenesis. Neither her "parents"
(Dark, Dawn) nor her son's "parents" (Herself +
water and sunlight) are deity-persons. They are
simply elements.

The mountain on which She was found as an
infant is sometimes referred to as the center of
the world. Reichard says of Her: (76, p. 407f)

Changing Woman is woman with a sphinxlike quality
. . . She is the mystery of reproduction, of life
springing from nothing, of the last hope of the
world, a riddle perpetually solved and perenially
springing up anew; literally expressed in Navajo

> . . . here the one who is named Changing Woman,
> the one who is named Whiteshell Woman, here her
> name is pretty close to the (real) names of every one
> of the girls. . . .

Changing Woman is usually "only verbally
described, unless the delineation of Earth in
sand painting represents her." (76, II, p. 407)
Reichard cites considerable evidence from the
myths to indicate the very close association
between Changing Woman and Earth and its rejuvenation. At one point in the Emergence myth
Changing Woman says, "There will be people, so
I cannot remain here and have myself tramped
upon." She is said to be decorated "with all
kinds of herbage and flowers wherever they
grew."

The descriptions of Changing Woman's
birth, childhood, adolescence, maturity, are
rich and beautiful. (See 60, 71) In them She
stands forth in her full stature as the dominant
deity.

> The tales imply that all creatures and powers bowed
> before Changing Woman. When Changing Woman
> came into the assembly of the gods, each one bowed
> his head. The sacred mountains bowed to the people
> returning from a visit, presumably to acknowledge
> the power of "their mother," Changing Woman. (76,
> p. 528)

Not only does She bear the divine hero
twins, destined to free the earth from monsters.
She also is described as having made the first
human beings from skin rubbed from various
parts of her body. Her cosmic cyclic movements
— aging each winter and becoming a beautiful

young maiden each spring — make Her the essence of death and rebirth, signature of the continual restoration and rejuvenation of Life.

She stands for peace and ever-renewed creation despite the fact that her twin sons are warriors. But theirs is war only of a certain kind. She says of them, in one of the great councils of the gods, "I did not bear these children to go to war, but to rid the world of monsters." (76, p. 407f) In this "war" aspect of the positive Feminine, it is needful to see that the "monsters" to be defeated can range all the way from our inmost darknesses and egocentricities to our outer most "infectious" non-responsibility for our planet's needs.

After Changing Woman separates herself from First Woman and First Man, She is innocently (magically, virginally) impregnated by sunlight and by water from a waterfall. Her twin sons, born from this impregnation, are named Monster Slayer and Child-Born-of-Water. She is considered Sun's wife (sometimes his second wife) and lives in the West, in a home which She at first refused, saying She might be lonely there.

In Matthew's version of the myth She asked that Her house be built on an island in the Western seas so too many people could not bother Her, and She requested animals for company, and so it was done.

Her gifts to people are rites and ceremonies. She is kind, gives songs, creates the horse, decrees fertility and sterility. Her presence at an assembly of the gods is deeply respected. After She destroyed many evil

powers by causing a fierce storm and told the
twins that no evil powers were left, Monster
Slayer found some, including Old Age, Cold,
Sleep. He could not destroy them, Changing
Woman told him, because they were something
in between good and bad.

Episodes in the life of Changing Woman,
from birth to puberty to pregnancy to old age in
a repeated cycle, could be multiplied on and on.
All are fascinating and dramatic, as is Changing
Woman Herself. Whiteshell Woman and Turquoise Woman are each identified with Changing Woman in rituals and ceremonies — turquoise and whiteshell being always associated
with Her.

The numbers two, four, and five are associated with Her. When human beings were created
at Her western home She gave them five pets
and five canes made from semi-precious stones.
With these canes (used always in ritual magic)
the people were able to strike water from the
desert. Her own power, always definitely divine,
is symbolized by the numbers two and four. She
cried for four days before She was found as an
infant on a sacred mountain. She grew to
maturity in twelve days. She bore twin sons.

When I talked with Fr. Berard Haile in the
hospital in Santa Fe shortly before his death, he
welcomed my questions about Changing Woman
and answered them fully. Despite his failing
health his spirit was bouncing. He said that,
although there are no Navajo words for "good"
as morally right and "evil" as morally wrong,
nonetheless Changing Woman (also her twins,

and possibly Talking God) was of a different kind of existence, he believed, from the existence of First Man and earlier beings. He also wondered if Changing Woman might be somehow oriental, or might show oriental influences.

Why does Changing Woman live in an ocean — or a beside-the-ocean — home, he wondered aloud. Why are Navajo so interested in the sea and in abalone shell? Did they not perhaps, in some ancient time, come across the Bering Straits? Is Changing Woman in any way kindred to Kwan Yin? Or to Amaterasu, Japanese creator goddess of the Sun?* Certainly Changing Woman is not lacking in compassion. But she is also a creator goddess.

*In Chinese myth Hsi Wang Mu, most widely known as "Mother of Heaven," is also called Mother of the Western Heaven. She is considered the feminine or Yin half of the original pair of deities. She was born of the Quintessence of Western Air. She lives in a magnificent palace of gold and jade, surrounded by enchanted gardens, orchards, jewel fountains. She resembles Changing Woman, for her abode, too, is in the West. Her jade resembles Changing Woman's turquoise. Both of their houses are described as beautiful and elaborate. Kuan Yin is the foremost Chinese feminine deity, and shows many similarities to Changing Woman. Two versions of her life are known, one from the Indian *Sutras* and one from the Sung period in China. In a very real sense She was a "changing" goddess, having gone through several death-birth metamorphoses before attaining Buddhahood. She lived on a sea-girt island after She became a goddess.

Amaterasu of Japanese myth is goddess of the Sun, counterpart of Susano-wo, her brother the Moon god (or sometimes Storm god). She is one of the Kami — gods generally benign. Although She was born from the left eye of the god Izanagi, who had entered hell to recover his dead wife Izanami, She is not sinister. She is goddess of sunlight, fruitful earth, and weaving — in the latter domain She resembles Spider Woman.

These provocative ideas and questions we exchanged that day cannot (yet, at any rate) be answered. Nor can I forget the alive concern of the dying priest who so loved the Navajo. Perhaps the fact that we asked the questions shows how remarkable Changing Woman is.

Even if no final answers can be given it is enriching to amplify Changing Woman's myth from other cosmological and mythological sources before exploring Her particular psychological-religious meanings.

The mythologies of Mexico and Mesoamerica — places which, as we have already stated, are thought by many anthropologists to have cross-fertilized the cultures of the Southwest — have goddesses similar in some ways to Navajo. Earth in its providing, nourishing, and often cruelly destructive aspects is their essential characteristic, while Spider Woman, Changing Woman, Snake Woman carry Her greater wholeness.

Lady Precious Flower of Mesoamerican myth, with her affinity for flowers and fruits and with her twins, is close to the symbolism of Changing Woman. Moreover, Lady Precious Flower is offered marigolds on the Day of the Dead — an obvious relationship to the sun and rebirth, a relationship shared by Changing Woman. Lady Precious Flower and Tozi, Our Grandmother, come nearer than other Mesoamerican goddesses to that Feminine which is benign (in life, death, and rebirth), good-giver, protector, eternal and eternally changing.

A comparison which seems very right to make is one between Changing Woman and White Buffalo Cow Woman from the great vision of Black Elk of the Sioux Indians. Black Elk said of her:

> . . . [I]t was the will of Wakan-Tanka, the Great Spirit, that an animal turn itself into a two-legged person in order to bring the most holy pipe to His people; and we . . . were taught that this White Buffalo Cow Woman who brought our sacred pipe will appear again at the end of this "world," a coming which we Indians know is now not very far off. (10)

She is first described appearing to two hunters as a mysterious and beautiful woman, dressed in white buckskin and carrying a bundle on her back. She announces that she comes with something of great importance. A ceremonial lodge is prepared for her, and within its ritual containment she presents the Sioux with a bundle containing the sacred pipe and a round stone. She tells them that with this sacred pipe they will walk upon the Earth, who is both Mother and Grandmother and who is sacred.

After the impressive ceremonial vision the beautiful woman leaves, and as she moves away from the people she goes through a series of changes — from woman to young red and brown buffalo calf, then to white buffalo, then to black buffalo, and finally after bowing to each of the four quarters of the universe, she disappears. White Buffalo Woman is Earth, and Earth

> is considered under two aspects, that of Mother and Grandmother. The former is the earth considered as

> the producer of all growing forms, in act; whereas
> Grandmother refers to the ground or substance of all
> growing things — potentiality. (10)

There are no other Feminine "goddess" figures, in my opinion, that come nearer, if as near, to Changing Woman in much of Her meaning as does White Buffalo Cow Woman.

Now let us go to Changing Woman Herself as She moves through the various Navajo chants and myths in all Her flowing fullness. She seems more gentle, quiet, and nonviolent than most of the Mesoamerican deities. Yet She has qualities in Her Feminine dimension which are richly inclusive.

She is related to all seasons and their alterations. She is related to the mysteries of birth and rebirth. She is protectress in Her role of helping to rid the earth of monsters. She has to do with creation, the sun, the earth, the western waters. The names of Her twin sons — Monster Slayer and Child-Born-of-Water — indicate the fullness of her inclusiveness.

What can She most represent to us who are non-Indian people in the contemporary world? (The ultimate mystery of any of these Holy Ones, including Changing Woman, can be fully realized only by those who have lived with them a lifetime. The rest of us, however, can try for the deepest understanding possible.)

How can we try to sense the inner meanings of Changing Woman? She the Changing — the encompassing of time and eternity, youth and age, birth, death, rebirth, forever moving and evolving — can we find this Feminine dimension of deity in our lives? Can we dare to risk that newer turn of the ancient spiral — that turn calling us to descend into a higher awareness of our substance and its spiritual direction? Can we risk following a She?

She is Earth and Sky. She is Lady of Plants and of Waters, with Her home by the sea. She is a creator, not only a bearer. Above all, She is an aspect of the Divine buried in the sands of our present deserts.

She is very akin to the mystical Feminine of the *Aurora Consurgens* — *Sapientia Dei* called a "divine feminine hypostasis," and said to be that "through which God becomes conscious of himself." Von Franz also describes this Wisdom deity as a "Feminine pneuma who enkindles and inspires . . . a feminine complement of the God-image itself . . . As an archetype, she is in fact form without limitation, eternal and yet manifest and repeatable in an infinite number of individuals." (90, pp. 155, 159, 165)

Had we known Changing Woman — Wisdom — deep in our hearts, would we have waged the wars we have? And with such weapons? She does carry the qualities of the Feminine half of the god-nature — qualities long lost from the religious attitudes of contemporary people.

Far too many of us behave as did the foolish Indian scout in Black Elk's vision of White Buffalo Woman. This scout did not recognize the beautiful and mysterious Feminine being as of the Great Spirit. He tried to possess Her by misusing Her, and was turned into a skeleton. She told the second scout to go to the people and

tell them She was coming to them to help them.

> And after awhile she came, very beautiful and sing-
> ing, and as she went into the tipi this is what she
> sang:
>
>> With visible breath I am walking.
>> A voice I am sending as I walk.
>> In a sacred manner I am walking.
>> With visible tracks I am walking.
>> In a sacred manner I walk. (62, p. 4)

This She is Earth, Sky, Plants, Seasons. She is holy, as Changing Woman is holy. Because She is breath and voice, She is also Spirit, Feminine Spirit, Holy Spirit, the Wisdom Feminine of the Old Testament, Ruach of Judaic thought, the Shekinah of the Cabbalists, Sophia of Gnosticism.

It might be well for us, living in our identical houses with our identical lives, under polluted skies on an exploited earth — it might be well if we could pray Black Elk's prayer, remembering especially these invocations:

> . . . You in the depths of the heavens, an eagle of
> power, behold! And you, Mother Earth, the only
> Mother, you who have shown mercy to your children!
>   Hear me, four quarters of the world — a relative I
> am! Give me the strength to walk the soft earth, a
> relative to all that is! Give me the eyes to see and the
> strength to understand, that I may be like you. With
> your power only can I face the winds. (62)

It is fascinating and encouraging to see how these self-same themes occur time and time again, in different clothes, in the dreams of modern people. A man struggling conscientiously to outgrow adolescent attitudes and to move into a more mature manhood, reported this dream:

> There was a princess and I was rowing across a lake to be with her. But then I was swimming a moat to reach a queen, very regal. I was to be in her service.

A woman in her sixties, moving toward the close of a fine professional career, dreamed:

> I am about to give birth. Two women doctors are with me, one younger and one quite old. I feel safe.

For both the man and the woman the Feminine changed greatly but remained essentially the same. The man was being asked to work for, to serve, his Feminine aspects in two different ways. How different this was for him from "pleasing mother." For the older woman, her own deepest Self as Feminine healing dimension was serving her. She was not being coddled, but delivered by the Changing Goddess. For each of these people the Feminine dimension was inclusive of youth and mature age and thus was encompassing change. Each Feminine facet would have different gifts and demand a different allegiance.

Knowledge of Changing Woman is complex, requires of us a wider vision than we suppose. She is a manifold complex of wife, widow, virgin, old woman, queen, princess, poisoner, healer, earth, wisdom, serpent, water. She changes as the moon changes. But such moon rhythms are not unpredictable.

There are many ancient goddesses who are "changing" in this way. The goddess of the Old Tigris-Euphrates culture had many names (i.e., Inanna, Ishtar, Aruru) and many sides. She too was virgin, was mother, was earth and nature; she descended to the nether world and returned again. So also with Greek Isis, and Demeter-Kore, and Kybele. But there are not many goddesses who are creators in the same way as Changing Woman is. She made human beings and looked after them subsequently.

Many goddesses are redemptive, presiding over birth, death, and rebirth. But not often do they preside over primal creation. Ge (Gaia), the oldest Greek deity, was said to have given birth to the heavens and thus "she was the creatrix of all things in heaven and in the world." (41, p. 230) Perhaps it can be assumed that every primitive earth goddess, as the inexhaustible source of all life, is in one way a creator. But few are described as such.

Changing Woman is unmistakably and totally the creator of human beings in Haile's _Emergence_ myth. She rubbed and rolled up skin from Her breast, back, arms, and armpits. She collected Jet, Turquoise, White Shell, Red-White Stone, Water Clay, Water Foam, Sparkling Sand, Water Pollen. She mixed these with Her skin, rolled the mixture into balls, and placed them in an Abalone Shell. She spread sheets of Turquoise and White Shell and on these She laid the mixtures She had made. An elaborate ritual followed, of covering, uncovering, covering, uncovering, singing songs (especially the

Woman Song), shaping living things. She made human beings, horses, sheep, dogs, chickens. When at last She removed the covering and saw they were alive, Changing Woman lifted a Dark Bow strung with a Rainbow and shot at them and "blew them beyond the ocean." (30, 59)

The Feminine Creator. How strange that sounds. Despite the He/She Creator in Egyptian myth and in at least one other Native American cosmogony, to encompass the fact that this She, this Changing Woman, made human beings *from Herself* requires a leap of both mind and heart away from preconceptions and established teachings. We expect the Word to precede the Substance, the rational and carefully tested Plan to be approved before the Product is released. Balls of skin and some semiprecious stones hardly seem adequate. But why do we expect evolving and changing life to come from a blueprint? Even in *Genesis* there are Jahweh, water, the abyss, and no plan.

But what is any more creative, in our various lives at various and unexpected occasions, than those feelings, thoughts, impulses, insights, solutions, and resolutions that arise in us out of a great and unplanned "Aha!"? It is not that a Feminine Creation is better (or worse) than a Masculine Creation. It is that both are necessary. Different but necessary. Changing Woman and Her Sisters are the Feminine Creators of time, movement, alteration and alternation.

The Acoma Pueblo creation tells of a primal goddess, Thinking Woman, with the Corn Mother under Her and twin sisters under Corn Mother.

The names of the sisters are usually translated as Bringing-To-Life and More-Of-Everything In-The-Basket. The two sisters each had a basket from which they drew out things which developed into people, animals, plants, etc. Their various works of serving the creation resemble in the small the work that was done by Changing Woman in making the world and the people in it.

As Changing Woman stands in the house of the Sun, She is described as Her twin sons saw Her:

> They saw a medium-sized woman who took a White Shell Cane in her hand and went east and returned much younger than before. She went south and her hair was gray when she came back. She went west and came back old and white-haired, and when she went north she went slowly and stopped. After this she looked at them awhile, and then she went east again, coming back as a beautiful maiden. (30)

Here is given the cycle of birth-rebirth, of spring to spring again, of the moods and seasons of living substance, of the rhythms of inner growth. Where Masculine creativity tends to move always forward, Feminine creativity tends to turn round on itself, not circularly so much as spirally. These two Creators — the Masculine and the Feminine — need to go hand in hand.

History, either of an individual or of a race, is in a very real sense irreversible. This year's spring is not last year's spring. Although I may have exciting new insights about myself, I am nonetheless growing physically old. But the creative ongoingness of the spirit of my living can — and does if I let it — proceed through its ever-renewing cycles until the very end of my life.

We have, as human beings, lost our aware-ness of Changing Woman as Creative dimension. We seem to go on the tacit, never-acknowledged assumption that re-birth and re-newal are absur-dities, and that therefore all we can do is to rush nowhere on our "indestructible" plastic wheels, devouring all substance and all experience before we end in nothingness. This is not necessary, not productive, not even finally true.

Astrophysicists have speculated and are even providing evidence for the fact that new universes are continually being "reborn" from imploding stars. So why not individuals? Women need to carry this Feminine renewal.

People who work deeply with their inner universes — poets, mystics, psychotherapists, fantasy writers, naturalists, painters, teachers, students, to name a few — are continually de-scribing in a variety of ways experiences of re-newal, re-birth, changing.

A patient told the following dream:

> I am with many people. We are acting out the sense and meaning of the Life Force. It is like a great Cosmic Child being born. There are long scenes of running, weariness, effort, to show this Birth.

The dreamer was male, but could as well have been female, for the dream content is asexual in its description of what individuals can do to remember and to relate to Changing Woman.

Each hour, each day, each year, we can move through Changing Woman's cycles if we will receive them. Even the sad words of a twentieth century ballad, "Where Have All the Flowers

Gone?" describe the cycle of flowers, young girls, young men, war, death, flowers again.

It is exciting and impressive to see what can happen to people of any age — young or well-advanced in years — when they open themselves to Changing Woman. Two dreams, the first from a person in the eighties and the second from a person in his thirties, show what I mean.

> I see five or six heads of men in an irregular arrangement. As I watch them, gradually they change into enormous flowers.

Her responses to life and to people and to herself were continually becoming softer and more loving and accepting. The dream said how it was for her, very clearly.

A man in the early thirties dreamed:

> I am shopping with L. (man friend) and A. (older woman friend) in a small grocery store buying supplies for the following days. We left and walked together westerly, toward a lovely sunset. A. was talking about a young woman we both knew, and about the struggles she had in her life. She said that the young woman had some friends who were "deathkins" because they did not face death squarely. As she said this we were going over the crest of a hill. When she said "deathkins" the perspective became abnormal as if to illustrate what was said, and when she said "face death squarely" the perspective again turned to normal and we went on.

For the young man, death was far off. And yet, having recently lost a parent, it was there to be dealt with, to be put into perspective. He himself said, when discussing the dream, "things become skewed if I let my deathkins come into things when I know they are invalid."

For both the old woman and the young man, Changing Woman brought needed alterations to their outlook on life, turned things around so that they could see more clearly the necessary attitudes for their lives. They could see because each had chosen to be on the life journey.

There are levels of changing journeys for each of us. Every psychological and spiritual journey forward has its infancy, its adolescence, its darknesses, its maturity, its old age, its death, its transformation. This movement is experience-able. It is Changing Woman.

To be created by Changing Woman (from Her own skin as the myth says) is to start from the sacred Feminine, from the place of "communion" and relationship and substantial fullness. Her breasts, armpits, and back make a horizontal and grounded mandala, a horizontal cross of creation. This aspect of the Feminine is creative changing, is the capacity to flow, is cyclic time, is earth and water, is a bringing together.

Here is a song from the *Creation Chant*. (34) The song is to help the one who is the subject of the rite to identify with the earth spirit — and vegetation is related to Changing Woman's yearly rejuvenation when She is born on a mountain. Thus the song truly belongs to Her, Changing Woman, and to Her in us.

> *It is lovely indeed, it is lovely indeed. . .*
> *I, I am the spirit within the earth;*
> *It is lovely indeed, it is lovely indeed. . .*
> *The feet of the earth are my feet;*

It is lovely indeed, it is lovely indeed. . .
The legs of the earth are my legs;
It is lovely indeed, it is lovely indeed. . .
The bodily strength of the earth is my strength,
It is lovely indeed, it is lovely indeed. . .
The thoughts of the earth are my thoughts,
It is lovely indeed, it is lovely indeed. . .
All that belongs to the earth belongs to me,
It is lovely indeed, it is lovely indeed. . .
I, I am the sacred words of the earth,
It is lovely indeed, it is lovely indeed. . .(76)

Snake Woman

Beautyway, or the myth of Snake Woman, seems to be the most apt conclusion to a book dealing with the Feminine for several reasons. First, it tells a journey of a heroine rather than a hero, and follows that journey to the conclusion of her initiation as a medicine woman — a high honor and part of a priestly function. It is also, as I see it, a myth of the Feminine descending into a marvelous web of the Feminine and Masculine intertwined — an event with close mythic parallels in some of the ancient tales of Demeter, Persephone, Ishtar, Innana, Amaterasu — all of whom as Feminine deities in various ways and for various reasons descend into a variety of underworlds.

Furthermore, this Navajo myth not only develops the shapes of human and divine struggles. It also relates in a vast and vague network of interconnections to myths of the Hopi and the Apache and to some of the already mentioned Serpent stories of Mexico and Central America.

This myth-ritual complex is related, as Haile (31) said, to "a state of harmonious being in the earth person, and perfect adjustment between the creative energy of the gods" and the earth people.

In the beginning the myth describes the dis-harmony, dis-ease. The myth-ritual complex is, then, for restoration of health, harmony, order — in short, for restoring beauty. It is accurate psychologically and impressive religiously — as old Navajo women and men have long known.

As has been said, sin for the Navajo is a state of imbalance, of dis-order. Healing therefore is restoration of a balance of opposites. Mental and physical health depends on getting things back into balance by relating to that aspect of deity from whom the greatest wisdom can come. The journey of Snake Woman into the underworld of the serpent power and back is the way of Femi-nine divinity. It is this, in the end, which restores beauty to the humans.

Beautyway is a companion myth to *Moun-tainway*. Both begin the same, then diverge at the point where two sisters follow different paths on their journeys. There are six more or less com-plete versions of *Beautyway*. We will deal with material from the most complete ones. (31)

I have found no single clear reason for call-ing this myth-complex *Beautyway*. In Navajo the word is related to words such as perfection, har-mony, goodness, or pleasant, good, worthy, ideal, holy, sacred. As with Navajo rituals gen-erally, so with *Beautyway*. It re-establishes order between people and gods — especially between people and the Snake gods.

Among the Hopi, there is a ceremony in which a Snake Maiden is brought into the rites of the Antelope Society to spend the entire night near the altar with the Antelope Youth. Waters (91, pp. 272-73) considers this to mean "a fusing of man's dual forces within the body of their common ceremonial for the one constructive purpose of creation." Tyler (86) discusses the Snake societies in several Pueblo ceremonies. He tells of a youth who makes a long and lonely trip down the great river, with many difficult events along the way. At the end he finds, and sleeps with, the Snake Maiden.

Mesoamerican myths have many serpent divinities, male and female. Cihuacoatl, Serpent Woman, is ruler of death and childbirth. The great Coatlique, a dominant goddess, has a skirt of serpents. There are other female and male snake deities in Mesoamerica, including the male divinity, Quetzlcoatl.

The Hopis and Zunis have a Horned Water Serpent who features in their early spring fertility ceremonies. This Serpent is portrayed in the ceremony by large, black and white, jointed and movable effigies. The largest one of them has many breasts and is called the "mother." (82)

When the Navajo myth of Snake Woman is approached, it, too, has a mysterious unknownness about it. (It is very old as a *Chantway*, containing certain songs and prayers from sources unknown to living medicine men and women, so that singers of the chants have had to learn the songs syllable by syllable.) It is embedded in Beauty, or Beauty Chant, or Beauty Chantway.

Lorenzo Hubbell of Oraibi, trader, helper and friend of the Navajo, reported (53) that *Beautyway* had a male half and a female half, and said that he had never seen the first half and believed it to be obsolete. Thus the female half, which will be considered here, is the one that is best known among the Navajo. It would seem that the Navajo *Beautyway*, whose major movements are downward, is an ordering of the relationships between the people and the predominantly chthonic and healing Feminine Holy Ones. Snake Woman becomes a healer.

This is the myth. A group of Navajo in old Navajo country are part of a war party sent out to get scalps of two Pueblo people, and whichever two Navajo warriors achieve this are to have two sisters of the chief as their rewards. Bear Man and Snake Man belong to the Navajo raiding party. The raid is a success. The scalps are found in the possession of "two old men about ready to die with old age. . . . One of these turned out to be Bear old man, while (the other) was Big Snake old man, they say." (31, p. 50)

The others in the war party object to giving the sisters to these two old men so a series of competitions of various kinds of arrow shooting are arranged, but the coughing, stumbling old men win each one of these.

A war dance is arranged. The two sisters, as was the custom, dance a circling dance around all the men at the feast, but do not include the old ones.

The girls grow tired and hot and wander to the river to cool off. They smell a sweet fragrance and see a mysterious light shining. "'From where does that sweet smell come, my younger sister! Suppose, sister, we step out to the edge of the people!' said the older of the two. 'Don't do it, my older sister. Is everything safe that smells? Don't do it!' she said."

However they do follow the strange light and the sweet smell. They come in the darkness to a place where there are two young men. These men, "talking to each other and in form fairly well grown, they found sitting there. With necklaces of heavy strands of slim white beads hanging about his neck and his earstrands dangling at the tip of them, the one sat there." (31, p. 57) The other is also well clad. Both have rich and beautifully made quivers, bows, and arrows. The girls sit down beside them and ask for some of the tobacco. After their fourth request they are given some. Then the girls crawl under the men's blankets and spend the night with them.

It is essential to know that, in earlier episodes of creation, Changing Woman asked Big Bear Man and Big Snake Man to care for her infant twins while she hunted for food. Also Bear and Big Snake were guardians of Changing Woman's home — as persons, as animal pets, and as protectors for the twins on their later travels. (76, pp. 264, 384) Reichard says Bear and Snake were "doubtless sent by Sun" to Changing Woman.

When day dawns, each girl sees beside her an old ugly man. Frightened and disgusted, they try to get free, only to find that they are literally tied to the old ones, Older Sister by a long and furry arm, Younger Sister by a big snake. Finally they succeed in breaking away. They run frantically, calling for their fathers but not finding them. (In some versions they are rejected by them.) Wherever the sisters run in their panic the smoke from the old men's pipes follows them magically.

(At this point the journeys of the two sisters separate, Older Sister's being told in *Mountainway*.)

Young Sister flees toward the west. She climbs mountains, trudges through mud and water, is stopped at one point by Endless Snakes, is helped by the Weasel People, but is always pursued relentlessly by Snake Man's tobacco smoke. She grows more and more tired and disheveled.

"Then, it seems, it happened that out of the trees some strange thing extended up which turned out to be the Black Rock. Over there a peal of thunder was heard, and as she was suffering from thirst, she thought she might be fortunate enough to find some water. So, it seems, she started out for that place. But she must have been a sight as she ran along." (31, pp. 63-64)

She goes to the top of Black Rock and then she sees a pool at its base and goes down to get a drink. A voice calls, "Shhh, shhh" four times. In vain, she looks about. At last she sees someone standing over her. "Some strange young man stood there, slim of form, painted with bluish white clay, his face painted, a skirt about him, with arm attachments, and a necklace and a rain plume. . . . He had many beads, they say." (31, pp. 65-66)

The handsome young man tells her that earth people shouldn't walk around here. She says she is fleeing an old man. He says that the old man doesn't know the way down in there where people are living. With his weasel skin pouch the youth taps against Black Rock at each of the compass points, and the stone tilts over and reveals a land below the earth. Out of the underearth a ladder extends, and wind rushes from the hole.

Younger Sister descends this crevice in the earth. As she walks in this lower land she is met by Mountain Sheep people and she plays with them. She wanders among ruins. She goes into a cornfield and picks corn.

She comes at last to the home of Snake People — although she does not seem to know where she is for some time. She is fed by them, in some versions. In one version she first makes cornmeal and cooks for them before they feed her. The old man from whom she has been fleeing enters the house unseen by her, and eventually (not in all versions) appears as the handsome young Snake Man to whom she is then wed.

In some versions, while she is staying with the Snake People and before she learns the rites, there is a series of happenings in which she disobeys instructions given her by the Snake People and has to be rescued and healed each time. Healing ceremonies are given for her — both for her original illness and for the misfortunes that befall her when she disobeys.

These ceremonies, given either by the Snake People or by Big Snake himself, are learned by her in all their complex details. (96)

In some versions she asks, or is asked, to return to her home and to teach *Beautyway* to her younger brother. One version (31, p. 115) says that the Snake People tell her, "You shall now start for your home. . . . These songs, with which you have become familiar in the past, and the prayersticks, prayers, and sand paintings, and ceremonies, all of which have become known to you, shall be of use to the earth surface people from now on and in time to come." Earlier they had told her that after the ceremony she would be "holy," that her body and the ceremony would become one. (31, p. 84) Thus She *is* in one sense *Beautyway*, is essentially deity.

While She is en route to Her former home She encounters a strange being, Owl, and learns very important additional medicine from him. (31, p. 120) He asks Her where She is going and why. She tries to avoid answering but he knows the answers already. He tells Her never to be in a hurry, to learn from every animal She meets, and to stop now and learn from him how to make incense, medicines, songs, sacrifices, and prayersticks belonging to Owl. She does so.

At last She returns to "home" — with (as) the full *Beautyway* rite, learned over a long period of time, and after many mistakes and great difficulties. She has been away four years. She meets Her former family of four — mother, father, two siblings. It takes Her four days (or months) to teach Her younger brother *Beauty-way*. It is a very elaborate and careful teaching. She teaches him the songs and prayers, the sixteen sand paintings, the making of the prayer-sticks for the gods. Four mornings they take ceremonial baths. Four days they work at the rites, singing all through the final night. At dawn they face the east and take the rites into themselves.

Snake Woman (as She is now called) bids Her former family farewell. (Or, in another version, She just stepped outside for awhile and then disappeared, leaving only a few tracks.) In any case, it is apparent that She returns to Black Rock and to the Snake People Holy Ones, to be reunited to them and in some way to Snake Man.

Reichard has written that "the Navajo does not count past blessings nor . . . give thanks in prayer . . . seeks not pity but correction. . . . The Navajo individual is the reason for the coordination of universal phenomena." Therefore ritual is directed from the individual outward towards tribal well-being. On this basis, *Beautyway* seems to be a psychological and religious myth-ritual complex concerned with disturbances and dis-harmonies either of the psyche or of outer situations — disharmonies marked by such things as outer illnesses or accidents, regressive behaviors of many kinds, fears of the irrational (of darkness, of death, of the dead), animal phobias, anxiety dreams of watery depths, reptile forms, earthquakes, and

the like. *Beautyway* can, in short, be as related to
outer and to inner disharmonies and their healing in Western European (particularly American)
individuals as it is related to Navajo — perhaps
more so.

As we non-Indians become ever more dangerously alienated from our Mother Earth and
thus from our own deep roots we are as individuals increasingly disharmonious, disunited,
distressed and disturbed. We are in need of healing in many dimensions.

The hypertrophied Masculine has discarded
— or has tried to discard — the irrational, the inner dream wisdom, the communion with earth
for itself, the enfolding of *all* life as necessary,
the letting happen of natural events, the lovely
recalcitrance of cyclic time, the ebb and flow of
inner and outer tides. An overpoweringly
Masculine world is discordant, is out of touch
with the Feminine world of rebirth and change.
Out of touch with Changing Woman. Out of touch
with that healing Feminine deity in a close-to-
human form, Snake Woman.

Dreams frequently mirror such disharmony
and discord and the need for restoration of an inner balance. Here are two dreams from a
modern, well-educated, non-Indian, "successful"
American:

> I'm driving my car fast down a steep hill. Then I'm on
> roller skates. Then I'm on foot with snakes coming at
> me from everywhere. I wake up terrified.

(A few months later.)

> I'm in a place under the sea. There are depths even below where I am. Porpoises and other big creatures are swimming near. I know I must go deeper and I feel afraid.

Even without further details about the dreamer, it is apparent that the dreams are pointing to a need for continual descent from technological heights to an ordinary place and thence to the religious depths.

Another dream, this from a younger but more "shattered" Third World American, shows again the descent theme:

> I'm wandering above deep deep seafoam green waters that are magnificently changeable. Sometimes a hole opens in them and a stream of liquid gold streams toward the center. Each step is made with terror and bliss. The danger of being engulfed is ever present but the mystery balances the fear. It is like walking on the highest and the deepest of waters at once.

Beautyway is also this sort of "dream" — of a singular journey over the earth to a place beneath the earth below the waters, to the place of Snake People — a place where balance is restored between earth and beneath-earth, between Feminine and Masculine, between enemies, between earth people and Holy people, one of them being Snake Woman.

Such dreams show a spiraling movement downward and an interweaving of opposites. The interplay of opposites in *Beautyway* is similarly stressed.

In one version of *Beautyway*, of the four men who start out for the sea and are drawn into the

Pueblo war, Frog and Turtle Man go back in fear, Bear and Snake Man go forward. That is, the slower and less aggressive representatives of the Masculine go in a different direction from the faster and more aggressive ones.

A pair of Masculine and Feminine opposites is found in the war party chiefs vs. the two sisters who are to be the prizes. Bear Man and Snake Man are Masculine but different, although both are chthonic figures as well as sky figures — especially if related to Sun. Older Sister goes up the mountain, and Younger Sister goes under the rock to the world of Snake People.

The myth itself is divided into the male chant of *Heavenly Beauty* and the female chant of *Earthly Beauty*. *Beautyway* thus encompasses Feminine and Masculine in such pairs as land and sea, fear and determination, male and female, heavenly and earthly, bear and snake. In the apparent power of the great warrior chiefs and the apparent feebleness of Bear Man and Snake Man the mythic route begins.

The journey told in *Beautyway* is for the achievement of inner and outer "beauty," of harmony between the individual and the god-energy. It is well to reemphasize this. Such a myth of a maiden, a sexual encounter, snakes, underworld, could be reductively interpreted as nothing but a message about sex and how to handle it in puberty. (This aspect of life is certainly included by Navajos.) But *Beautyway* is far more than that, and to reduce it to its least and narrowest is to do it a grave disservice. We can do no less than grant a high regard to *Beautyway* as we try to find its meaning for us.

In the beginning of this myth, war and aggression and scalping are the dominant actions. By the Navajo definition, which generally makes Masculine active and heated, the Masculine dimension is the major manifestation. The War God Hero Twins head the war party. (Child-Born-of-Water has some Feminine elements, to be sure.) The "enemy" are Pueblos — a relatively quiet and agricultural people in fact — and the trophies sought are usually named as scalps of Pueblo virgins. So the Feminine is on the defensive.

After Bear Man and Snake Man win the scalps, the many other suitors for the sisters and the many shooting contests to decide who may have the sisters add weight to the already top-heavy Masculine. At this early stage of the myth, action is largly thrust, hostility, chauvinistic competition. It is also the Masculine in its more adolescent phase.

Such adolescent Masculine attitudes mark a great deal of our late childhood and early adolescence — males and females alike. The bully, the tomboy — these roistering, argumentative, and competitive mannerisms can be recognized as belonging to the young of all warm-blooded species including the human.

In their proper chronology these attitudes are right and natural. However, they can be seen at other ages of life and are not so natural and fitting when they outlive puberty.

For Navajo, Black Rock is an island in the desert, with water at its base. (In some versions, a lake.) Black Rock is believed by some to mark the place of Emergence so sacred to the Navajo

— the place where the first beings emerged from the lower worlds.

Islands as places surrounded by water (oceans, oceanic deserts of sand) are realms of mystery, magic, danger. If their surroundings are generally symbolic of the unknown, hard-to-endure-god-realm, then the islands symbolize places of groundedness from which a person may better deal with the darkness and unfamiliarity and threat of the unconscious.

The following dream — belonging to a woman of 40 emerging anxiously from immaturity into an entirely uncharted phase of her life — shows how the unconscious "chooses" figures from the Navajo myth (completely unknown to the dreamer) in order to help the growth process:

> There was a serpent coming. I can't remember the details. Then there was a scene where a whole group of women are being instructed in a dance which leads out into a desert. Then I am pursuing a large black spider, almost the size of a small dog. I have great fear of it but I overcome my fear and befriend the spider and bring her with me. This was an extraordinary thing.

If we then see such dreams as relating to the world inside us — to the inner deities (Spider Woman, Snake Woman) — perhaps they can help us to help that world.

This woman feared snakes as too much phallic Masculine (as her father was), and spiders as devouring Feminine (as her grandmother had been). The dream touched her deeply because she felt that the snake was leading her — and other women — into the dance of life. And the spider as friend became an "enchantment," she said. Out of this dream she became aware of doing things more "serpentinely," indirectly, gently, as a dance. And she could accept the "weaving feminine" for the first time.

At an opposite place with regard to the "snake" symbol is a young and very unconscious woman, too easily offering herself as a sexual partner to men and cut off from her deeper femininity as a quality to be honored. She dreamed:

> I was with my sister and brother. I had made a big bottle of a chemical mixture for something. As we crossed the lawn of the house I saw a hole. We decided it might be a gopher and poured the mixture down. A huge black worm emerged, became a snake, and as it kept coming it got longer and longer, to about twenty feet. We ran into the house but he chased us. He looked very angry. He chased my mother, then my sister and me. My brother tried to push the snake out but he bit my brother. At last the snake got disinterested and went back to his hole.

This young woman had a very difficult time facing her problems, especially with regard to her own poor self-image and her use of men as ways to make her feel more worthwhile.

At a very different place, in terms of self-regard and self-insight, was a woman who was deeply into her own "rebuilding," as she called it. Her dreams truly told where she was:

> I was in a large building and a big green serpent was kept in a room upstairs, or in an attic. The serpent was not unfriendly, but he had to be fed or otherwise he might attack. I was with the serpent and realized the owners had not fed him for several days. I knew he

> was dangerous in his hungry state and knew I must
> feed him.

She had a right inner sense that this "serpent power" had to be honored and cared for, that it must not be left hungry and angry.

A third person, more mature than the other two and much deeper into the inner work of wholeness, dreamed:

> I see a small tree, with a trunk and boughs graceful
> and like a miniature elm. The branches and trunk are
> golden with heart-shaped translucent leaves. It is
> covered with dew and alive with the movement of
> many small silver snakes. This is a living symbol of
> the balance of silver and gold, the result of a struggle
> between owl and serpent.

In the *Beautyway* story, after the beginning successes of the war party and the securing of the trophies, the plans of the dominant Masculine characters break down. When Snake Old Man and Bear Old Man turn out to have the scalps, the chiefs are upset. They try again to impose their rules by setting up arrow-shooting contests — and incidentally by summarily breaking the first agreement. But the miserable old men win the arrow-shooting contests nonetheless.

The Masculine power of the establishment is not winning out despite the chief's efforts — a situation not unknown to us today. It is exactly at this point that the Feminine begins to be seen as more than just two sisters at the mercy of the Masculine rulership. Our first sight of it is very indirect and mysterious and almost hidden.

In the description of the two scalps, which to the dismay of the warriors were held by Snake Old Man and Bear Old Man, one scalp is described as being "smooth with turquoise" and the other as being "smooth with white shell beads." These colors and sacred stones belong to Turquoise Woman and Whiteshell Woman, or to Changing Woman, who is essentially these two combined. Thus almost from the beginning the Feminine deity of "changing" is included subtly in the theme of the upsetting of one-sidedness and dis-harmony.

Furthermore the first and decisive break with rules comes from the two sisters. As aspects of the Feminine they have been subject to the disposition of the warrior Masculine, have been given as prizes, have been shunted from war to shooting contests and finally to the dance, and have been manipulated by the fathers.

For a time the sisters obey the Masculine command, dancing their customary circling dance around all the possible male suitors. But when they grow tired of this it is they who take matters into their own hands and wander away in the night to the dark river. At that moment of their choice, father domination is breaking and, despite further tries at patching it up, it remains broken.

One woman, married, with children — in the eyes of the world seemingly doing very well in life — was quite cut off from her deeper Feminine nature. Her mother had been power-driven, and had given to her daughters very little real understanding or acceptance of Feminine sexuality.

The woman was beginning, however, to realize how cut off she was from natural responses. She had this dream:

> I live by the ocean. I am going home. There are many children around. Before I get there I see a group rushing by with two girls — one screaming — and soldiers — one naked — and he has raped the girl. I run into my home. An unknown old woman sits there quietly. She looks at me, smiles, and says that there are unusual earth lines showing an important mystery.

She had to face the fact that the Feminine had been "raped" by her mother's militant rationalism, and that what she (the dreamer) needed now was to hear "the old woman of the earth mystery" — as she called her.

If the Feminine is to become co-worker with the Masculine in the balanced way of the Navajo, it has little chance until the one-sided dominant patriarchal dimension ceases to be able to hold its rule. From the moment the two sisters smell the beguiling tobacco fragrance, hear the alluring and unfamiliar sounds, see the mysterious light gleaming in the darkness, and move toward these imperatives — from that moment a new world begins. The snake is being fed rightly.

In one aspect this movement is not so very far from the early descriptions in the book of *Genesis* of the "disobedience" of the first created beings. To be sure, the two sisters had not been told *not* to sleep with strange men. They had been told to choose husbands from those men around whom they were dancing. But they did not stay with the wishes of the patriarchal

Masculine. Again, like the first beings in Genesis they were drawn by sensory lures. Eve "saw that the tree was good for food, and that it was a delight to the eye." (RSV Gen. 3:6)

Through the ears, eyes, noses, the two girls were drawn to a new level of existence. Probably for the first time in their lives the two sisters were able to extricate themselves from the paternal order. The Feminine, drawn by its own desire, says Yes to the unknown and No to the usual expectation. This night spent with Bear Man and Snake Man is only the beginning of a much longer one for the young women — a journey which ends in feminine shamanism, healing arts, and Feminine deity.

The foundations of *Beautyway* are laid in this first movement of the Feminine from patriarchal world toward medicine woman (priestly) status. This must not be forgotten. Yet neither must sexuality be forgotten.

The Feminine becomes now the active principle rather than the acted-upon. The two sisters find the young men, keep importuning until they are given the sweet smoke of *eros* and, bewitched by the unconscious and alluring shadow side of the Masculine, choose to spend the night in love.

In addition to saying that sexual outreach is as much of the Feminine as of the Masculine, what else is the myth saying? Perhaps that the Feminine has its own kind of psychic demand for the quality of enfoldment. Perhaps that the magnetism of the senses somehow belongs to the Feminine more than to the Masculine. Also that Feminine and Masculine do in fact seek one another not only in deity but in every healthy psyche in order to bring about wholeness. Here the smoke has the function of joining together, of continually drawing Feminine toward Masculine.

Smoke has always had *mana* for American Indian groups. It is related to fire, to communication, to medicine pipes, to blessing. In Navajo myth it is associated with "creation, clouds, war, power, and purification." (76, p. 598) In short, it indicates major activity for change. In alchemy, smoke is also a symbol of changes and transformations.

When the sisters follow their own emotional desires and are finally forced into the unexpected situation, it leads to transformations. For each sister a young man became an old man — and ultimately the old becomes young.

Where can we recognize such workings of the Feminine? We find it in the senses — in the response to and reach for color, taste, fragrance, texture, sound, qualities of touch. Anyone who responds intensely to these various stimuli is using and being used by the Feminine. The novels *Germinal* (Zola) and *The Remembrance of Things Past* (Proust) involve male characters in the attitude of the sense-responding Feminine. Writers, painters, sculptors — these artists especially — are well-known for their ability to use the Feminine intensely.

Not only is the sensorium always requiring of the artist, but also there is an urgent sensitivity towards the inrush of perceptions. Rilke wrote in a letter that "the deepest experience of the creator is feminine: for it is experience of receiving and bearing." (79, p. 181) This is true. It is equally true that this Feminine as it functions in the artist is actively seeking to "receive" from the artist.

And to "bear" is the playful hard work of art. Another poet said of her father, "He worked as poets work, for love,/And gathered in a world alive." (81, p. 103) Thus the artist includes the Feminine attributes of changing, enfolding, esthetic response, and communion.

This creative and sensuous awareness is available to all who will open to it, as the sisters opened to it. Perhaps these aspects of Feminine so necessary to artists are equally necessary to enable any of us to respond to art, or to risk being imaginative, or to "follow our noses" as children or animals do. We can learn much about ourselves if we risk thus opening out — even in such small and difficult ways as to go by ourselves and move to music, or to draw or paint the way we feel, or to work with a lump of clay.

The contemporary American, English, and Nordic subcultures actively stressing "sensory awareness" of various kinds are, in part, relating to the sense-responding Feminine. (However, some of the activity that passes for "sensory awareness" turns out to be sexual titillation and exploitation, and is not Feminine so much as it is a one-sided Masculine seeking to have manipulation powers.)

To recapitulate: we have at this point of the myth Feminine deities drawn away from dominant patriarchal gods. How many adolescents, girls and boys alike, in the first splendid defenselessness of being in love with life are moved into this situation. An older generation — which always exists — says they are "silly," not recalling its own "silly" times.

The young forget their tasks. They wander in the night. They write poetry. They pick up shells, flowers, stones, feathers, and sleep out under the stars beside fires. They stumble into primal mysteries — sex and other "creation" — hardly knowing what they do. Yet they are trying to touch deity, to find a "beautiful orderliness," even if their success is relatively limited because they have not yet the courage for what they seek.

As with the sisters, so with any of us. The awakening is not as we had expected. In the bright dawn, what Younger Sister saw (and we will discuss only her journey) was not the beguiling youth of the night but an ugly old man to whom she was tied by a long snake. Enchantment this may be, but of a seemingly obnoxious and sinister kind. The original patriarchate has been replaced by something seen as much uglier and less rational.

The first response to such a distasteful outcome of having risked disobedience is to run for cover. We want the Masculine patriarchate once more to hide us, protect us with its laws, tell us what to do now. However, this relation has already been severed. The "beauty" of the mysteries of the darkness — scents, sounds, colors — will not let us go.

It is as if the word "tied" (as Younger Sister was tied to the old man by the snake) had a much deeper meaning. We usually use "tied" in a more or less negative sense. We say someone is "tied" to children, to spouse, to work, to an idea —

meaning that they are "dependent upon for validation," are "enslaved by."

But "tied" also means "related to," "equal to," "being conditioned by" — in the sense perhaps that humanity is "tied" to its planet and its planet's atmosphere, etc. Younger Sister was first negatively "tied" to the Masculine Father. From her awakening onward she was "tied" to a quite other aspect of a greater power, as Juliana of Norwich wrote of being "tied by a leash of longing" to God.

We touch something new, sweet, creative, exciting, mysterious. In the intuitive and misty darkness of unknowing it seems right and true. When we look closely we recognize that there are other aspects of reality (i.e., old age, ugliness, tasks) to be faced. Objectivity is not so easy.

The Masculine as an equal to the Feminine seems too harsh. We are reluctant and afraid. We want the all-knowing and paternalistic Masculine to help us. It is fortunate for us if we cannot find this Father God, then, if we are forced as younger Sister was to lift our own scared life and move on. And men as well as women — or women as well as men — want the Feminine dimension to remain under the dominion of the father Masculine.

Situations of trying to triumph over another, trying to have the upper hand, are flights from the Feminine try-for-understanding (which takes more time) to the Masculine I-am-top-dog weaponry. Younger Sister tries this kind of flight when she calls for her father. Fortunately, she cannot get to him.

Thus Younger Sister, either rejected by or unable to find the father, flees westward, continuing in the direction Snake Man had originally been going. She has a difficult and harsh journey, first through deserts and then through much mud and water.

Water world, sea and sands, liquid earth — how often these are described in myths of beginnings. In Matthews' story of the Emergence there is water in all directions. Genesis tells of the Spirit of God moving over the waters.

It is difficult to determine clearly what the meaning of the serpent goddesses was to the Mesoamerican culture and to the Pueblo groups. It seems to mean something between good and dangerous. It seems also to relate to fertility in some fashion, but it (or She) holds itself wrapped in an air of mystery.

The Mayan *Popol Vuh* describes the waters in which the Forebears rest to plan creation. Maori myth has the gods in darkness and water.

There are numerous myths where some small creature (duck, turtle, etc.) must go down into the waters to bring back a bit of wet earth for creation. In these instances the water is "the unformed, unstable and pregnant reality . . . the uncreated . . ." (54, p. 192) Younger Sister's arduous journey deposits her at just such a place to face a new creation.

The *Popol Vuh* (29) has an episode of a maiden, Xquic (blood of a woman), who is similarly torn between opposites. Xquic, however, begins in the underworld as daughter of a lord of the underworld. She is impregnated by spittle from the skull of a man who had come from the upper world. She flees the wrath of her father and gets to the upper world. There she lives with the mother of the dead man — an old Earth Mother — and bears twin sons. They eventually descend to the underworld, defeat the lords of the underworld, and return to the upper world.

Xquic is a combination of Eve, the serpent, and Mary. She brings Feminine creativity from the underneath levels of being to more consciousness — as does Younger Sister at the end. Both of them as deities bring dark and light together. Both of them are served by owl guardians. Neither is only an Earth Mother figure. Each carries the Feminine aspect of deity as a bridge to expanded awareness, although in different ways.

To return to Younger Sister's journey: she has been running for very long both from paternalistic domination and from the seductive and terrifying opposites of Snake Man. When she can go no further, overcome by fatigue and thirst she stops at Black Rock (in the myth obviously a place related to ancient cliff dwellers). At this place she hears the call of the young man.

Once more the Feminine chooses to listen to and thus to enfold — as it chose to follow the sweet smoke in the beginning. As Eve also chose the unknown. In a similar way Rebekah chose disobedience to the patriarchal Masculine in order to help the younger Masculine find a new heritage.

Something rocklike is what the Feminine in us needs most at such a time of fatigue, illness, loneliness, fear, and confusion. It is an unknown place to which we come, to be sure, and yet it is at least a place of boundaries given by the rock, of rest and respite given by the water. As Younger Sister stands there confused, wet, her clothes torn, she hears the gentle call of the young man who cautions her and at the same time opens the earth for her to descend into another world.

It is apparent from later events that the young man is sending her down to Big Snake Man's realm — and that he knows what he is doing, despite his statement to the contrary. He is himself, almost certainly, Snake Man in youthful form. The weasel pouch he wears and uses to open the earth is important in later rites as having positive curative power. Its use here seems to indicate that Younger Sister *must* descend in order to learn healing and become deity.

It is not an easy "must" to say yes to because, in the words of a character in a modern play, "to approach the stranger is to invite the unexpected, release a new force, or let the genie out of the bottle. It is to start a train of events beyond your control." (27, p. 28) The Feminine has now moved totally from its subservience to the aggressive father Masculine to a willingness to follow the cyclic way of descent and ascent, death and rebirth, and to go in its own way through the waters of the *deus absconditus* (hidden god). The Feminine has followed the senses and it cannot return to the father dominance, but also it cannot escape having to face and learn the needs of the chthonic Masculine deity (Snake Man).

These opposites, Younger Sister Feminine deity and Snake Man Masculine deity, have been tied together since their beginning on that fateful "morning after." Now they must somehow be reconciled, reunited, enfolded as a totality at this central place.

In Navajo symbolism, snakes stand for the connection of earth with subterranean waters. For a culture such as ours — dominated by a one-sided Masculine attitude perpetuated by generations of males who assumed their primacy, and generations of females who countered male primacy by their sexual-matriarchal "mother" domination — this reconnecting is deeply needed. Our Judeo-Christian myth begins with a snake and a "fall" into relatedness. The Navajo myth goes, by way of a descent to the snake, forward to relatedness and healing.

In Kundalini Yoga the devotee in the beginning "imagines the divine power (*Sakti*) as being asleep within him, withdrawn from operation in his gross physique, coiled away like a sleeping serpent (Kundalini) at the root of his spine." (101, p. 33) The snake must be awakened by the devotee. Then the snake moves upward from the lowest center (chakra) to the highest. In the Navajo myth also there is first a descent from ego consciousness to the depths and then an ascent. The ancient tales of caverns underground and goddesses and oracular priestesses who have serpents as familiars are still living in this

Navajo myth. Thus *Beautyway* points us back to many ancient parallels.*

In a personal conversation with Dr. Jung many years ago, he told me of his first encounter with a cobra on a safari in the East. It was, he said, numinous and fear-producing because it was so wholly other, so not-human in any way, so ultimately mysterious. This is why, he believed, the serpent had such power and such *mana*.

In discussing the great snake in Pueblo Indian myth and ritual, Tyler points out that it is "not only a powerful beast . . . . but is as well one who has recourse to the underworld where the dead live. . . . As such it may be an ancestor. . . . Since the snake can kill, it can also

---

*In Egypt the cobra goddess Buto was defender of the pharaoh, was called "she who supplies cool water," wore the uraeus serpent crown of Lower Egypt. At the shrines of Minoan Crete there are many representations of the dominant goddess with snakes coiled around arms and body, snakes hand held, snakes moving from the goddess to feeding bowls. At Gournia, Crete, the Snake-goddess was "the chthonic Earth-mother in the dual aspect of the Goddess of fertility and the Mistress of the nether regions." (41, pp. 129-31) Athena, warrior goddess and protectress of Athens and related also to wisdom and the arts, wore serpents on her shield. Also in Athens there was a legend which said that one ruler's soul, after death, lived on as a snake in the Erictheon on the Acropolis. Gaia, ancient of Greek goddesses, was called a "pythoness" and lived at Delphi. Apollo slew the pythoness but afterwards she, either as snake or woman, became the soothsayer, the Delphic oracle. (Medusa had serpents on her head — a negatively dark aspect of Feminine dimension.) In India the goddess Kali in her darker manifestation is encircled with snakes. The snake in myth can heal and help and, through a new skin, can bring immortality.

cure. In its role as communicator between the upper and lower world, it knows of seed and fertility." (86, p. 221f) It is related to lightning and rain as well as providing a cure for snakebite. It has supernatural powers.

Great Snake — for Southwest Indians, Mesoamerican Indians, Northwest Indians — is of immense importance. Stephen, in a book on the Hopi Indians (83, p. 102), says that this Serpent has dominion over the earth's waters. According to Barbeau (6, p. 231f), the Dragon-serpent has "traveled the world," from ancient Asia to China, Japan, India, Polynesia, and to the Kwakiutl Haida of North America as well as throughout Europe.

Generally this snake form is many-headed, often fire-breathing, and usually threatening and to be destroyed. It has been assimilated as a more beneficent power as the Plumed Serpent of Mayans, Aztecs, Iroquois-Huron groups, and as the Rain God of the Southwest. It is probable that the serpent symbol always was positive at the beginning, only becoming negative as people became separated from its meaning.

Bancroft, writing a century ago and thus being a hundred years nearer than we are to the Native American groups, left a splendid statement regarding the serpent:

> As another symbol, sign, or type of the supernatural, the serpent would naturally suggest itself at an early date to man. Its stealthy, subtle, sinuous motion, the glittering fascination of its eyes, the silent deathly thrust of its channeled fangs — what marvel if the foolishest of men, like the wisest of kings, should say, "I know it not; it is a thing too wonderful for me?" It

seems to be immortal; every spring-time it cast off and crept from its former skin, a crawling unburnt phoenix, a new animal. . . . It does not appear that savages attach any special significance of evil to the snake, though the presuppositions of early writers almost invariably blind them on this point. (5, p. 134)

Jung also emphasized this, adding in his statements the relationships between snakes and souls and numina, snakes and spirits of the dead, snakes as guardians and givers of second sight, snakes and Mercury, snakes and healing.*

*The earth deity Coatlicue of Mesoamerican culture with Her encircling snakes is an "enigmatic figure," and Nicholson quotes a description from Torquemada, probably taken down verbatim from an Indian informant:

Though you may know me as Quilaztli (germinating principle or edible grass), I have four other names by which I am known. One is Cuacihuatl, which means Mother Snake; another Cuahuicihuatl, which means Mother Eagle; another Yaocihuatl, Mother Warrior; the fourth Tzizimichihauatl, which means Mother of the Inferno. And according to the attributes included in these four names, you see the power I have and the evil I am able to do to you.

Nicholson then quotes this poem about Coatlicue:

The Goddess is upon the rounded cactus:
she is our Mother, Obsidian Butterfly.
O, let us look upon Her.
She is fed upon stag hearts in the Nine Plains.
She is our Mother, Queen of the Earth. (69)

Nicholson further cites a description of the great statue of Coatlicue in the Museum of Anthropology in Mexico City: "The whole of her vibrates and lives, inside and out, the whole of her is life and is death; her meaning stretches in all possible directions . . . Coatlicue is the dynamic-cosmic force which gives life and is maintained by death in

When the young man opens the earth and shows another level of existence to Younger Sister and she chooses to descend and is not deterred by winds and strangenesses, it is the Feminine proceeding from an "exhalation" of the too familiar Masculine to an "inhalation" of the unknown. In these depths She discovers unexpected nourishment, a new family, and the power to become a healer.

Many women — and some men — are required by newer demands of the inner journey to make this descent-ascent. The following series of dreams belongs to a mature woman well along in her understanding of herself, and deeply committed to increasing that understanding. The dreams came within a six month period.

> (1) I'm outdoors, looking over a cliff down into a canyon. The canyon floor seems far away but not too far to get to. It is quite gray, and feels a bit eerie. Strange animals are wandering around, especially horses. They come out from caves. There are growing things there — but grayish. I make a statement about death being there. One person goes down through a fence. Is there danger? I must go.

the struggle of contraries which is so necessary that its final and most radical meaning is war . . . Thus the dramatic beauty of Coatlicue has ultimately a warlike meaning, life and death, and that is why she is supreme, a tragic and a moving beauty." One other fascinating development of the serpent is to be found in Gnosticism, especially among the Naasenes and Ophites, where Sophia is seen as the serpent and where even Mary is sometimes related to serpents.

(2) I am sitting at a table with three women. One woman is telling the second woman what the third woman, a Japanese, has given us for gifts. She is stressing how creative the relationship has been for all of us three and this Japanese woman, and says that we need an interpreter to communicate this to her.

(3) With another woman I enter a small, darkish house. The woman whose house this is (and whom we are coming to see) greets me warmly and embraces me. I feel I should be greeting her — but I become aware that she has been waiting a long time for me. I am surprised. There is now a fourth woman in the room. I become aware then that there is another beautiful room next to the one where we are. It is empty of people but has beautiful rugs and bookcases in it. The fourth woman is an artist and is welcoming me to a creative life I had not expected.

This remarkable series of dreams illustrates richly some of what the descent of Snake Woman in us involves. For this dreamer the first dream pointed to a descent into unknown aspects of herself — shadowy, eerie, dangerous perhaps — but aspects that held life as well as death. Then she is in a quaternity of Feminine — including her own ego-being — and is now aware of the need to understand a "foreign" (Japanese) part of her nature. And, finally, another quaternity of Feminines makes it clear to the dreamer that she must reach into the depth of her own artistic creativity and open to its unexpected richnesses.

This world below the known one can be understood as any mysterious and unknown depth into which we must descend — sexuality, dreams, psychological-religious commitment, even death itself. Overall it is the spiritual death-rebirth cycle essential to healing. It is terrifying and infinitely rich.

Let us recall again the manner of the Feminine in us as it has manifested in *Beautyway*. It moves from passivity to choice, from above to below, from "female dependency" to medicine woman (priestess deity). The Feminine makes the descent. This is becoming more and more true today. Women stepped forward to restore the Feminine to its rightful place by taking the lead in being more open to "descend" into the healing inner world. For quite a few years most groups exploring ways of psychological-spiritual inwardness had a preponderance of women. Men tended to consider it "weak" and/or "unscientific" to become involved in such interests.

Today there is a much more open attitude with regard to the non-rational, the world of the unconscious, the world of religious experience and religious commitment and communion, defined as a part of the Feminine way. When a male college student of mine — a fine athlete — told me desperately that he wanted more expression for his "feminine side" my hope for the future was considerably enlarged.

Of major importance to our present world and its complex and growing problems is the social meaning of *Beautyway*. We stand naked and empty and (hopefully) afraid. It is the Feminine deity who needs to be honored now above all, for She holds the possibilities of creative earth power, of enfolding, letting happen, knowing compassion and desiring communion on earth. Our planetary journey was for too long only upward and outward. All the way to the moon and Mars.

We are now at that place in the myth where She stands lonely and tired and dirty. And we too are, as Snake Woman was, confronted by the serpent power with the choices of flight from it, fight with it, or descent into the world it shows to us. To let Snake Man tilt the rock and lead Younger Sister Feminine deity down into the medicine place would be for us (men and women alike) to open ourselves to newer, quieter, gentler, more sensitive and deeper solutions in our lives. They will not necessarily be easy solutions, nor will they be painless and safe. They will be re-solutions, involving entering into depth, death, cyclic time, re-birth, relationship of a different kind to new aspects of Feminine, inner and outer.

Many dreams, as we have seen, indicate what is involved in this new kind of action. Three more contemporary examples may serve. The first belongs to a young professional man in his thirties:

He dreamed he was in the country with a seminar group to "study inner things." He and a male friend, needing to urinate but finding all toilets occupied, went into the woods. Just as they were about to relieve themselves a large serpent entered the woods "like a clap of thunder. We stepped aside to let her pass. She wore a rust and brown bonnet, a robe of the same color, and came intently past us, a deeply concerned expression on her face." The dreamer said he felt the snake was a Feminine power of earth and life to which everyone had to listen. At the same time the serpent also made him think of a very dear woman friend — much older than he — who had often given him "common sense advice" about his daily life.

The second dream comes from an older woman, also in professional work:

> I am with many people on an island surrounded by vast seas, held back by natural reefs and manmade barriers. I am deeply impressed by these seas and high waves. It is almost as if we had climbed to this place from beneath the earth. Some of us are stroking lovely young animals of endangered species. It feels as though all the world was on this great island, either trying to live in peace or fleeing. It was either beautiful or awful, filled with wonder or terror. Somewhere I say to another, "I will not let you go until you bless me."

The dreamer said she felt this was both her predicament and the world's, and that all people had to see and work with and be healed by the wonder of it, or live running and afraid.

A young woman who had been, as a child, very negatively caught and dominated by a too strong father, was working intensely to free her inner child from her fear of this father. She was beginning to feel a sense of her own validity. A dream stated it this way:

> I am in a place of parts with powers. They seemed like serpents — five of them — two at home, two elsewhere, and one that communicates between. And there is also a child with power — a girl — not under a father's power.

Such inner experiences reflect the deep need for a new kind of encounter with chthonic deities, and are therefore similar to the journey of Younger Sister as she moves down into the

land below. The place of Emergence, or our earliest beginnings, has to be courageously entered
again if any re-solution and re-birth is to come.
Our Feminine must let itself be guileless and
naive, free from the traps of Masculine "scientific truth" and "success." This guileless openness permits us to embrace the myth's "others"
— the ruins and cornfields and corn and Mountain Sheep deities (related to harvests, plenty,
seeds) and eventually to the Snake deities in
their own place.

Younger Sister's direction from this point on
is towards the eventual priestess-deity status. In
this movement, the approach of Feminine and
Masculine aspects of deity to each other grows
clearer. They are equally needed for healing,
wholeness, "beauty." Younger sister needs both
Snake Man and Owl to teach her to be a medicine
woman. Snake Man and the Snake people need
her to learn the rites in order to teach them to
the earth people, and to teach *Beautyway* to the
brother. The earth people — all of us — need her
to pass on the healing arts and the capacity for
wholeness learned by her in the death-rebirth
journey.

In many alchemical works the essential
role(s) of the snake leap out in rightness. The
feminine figure descends into the dragon-toad
world. Dead souls and numina appear as snakes.
Snakes are guardians and givers of second sight.
Snakes are related to the hermaphroditic Mercury, to the moon, to the underworld, to the
caduceus and healing, and to the *uroboros*
which surrounds the world.

For Younger Sister to become Snake Woman is for the incomplete Feminine to become completed by a relationship both to the youthful Masculine and to the mature Masculine (through both the younger brother and Snake Man in his two manifestations).

From a man's inner point of view, Snake Woman is that Feminine in him most deeply needed to complement his Masculine nature (whether it is strong or weak). If it is strong, it profits from a gentling. If it is weak, it profits from the strength of the younger brother's knowing of the rites.

From a woman's inner point of view, this journey of Snake Woman is every woman's journey to become her true Self, separated from all stereotypes of what she "ought" to be. If she has had a weak father, she may be struggling with her own compensatory Masculine power drive. On the other hand she may be sinking beneath the lake of insecurity. If she had an overly aggressive or patriarchal father, this devaluation is apt to occur. She is then gravely in need of communion with her whole Feminine nature. Snake Woman's movements — seen within each woman's psychic being — can enrich and restore the Feminine.

At the (temporary) end of the long road from First Woman to Snake Woman — with all the in-between dimensions, negative and positive, of the Feminine deity — the unknown road into the future disappears. It is to be hoped that this wisdom of the Pueblo and Navajo people, transmitted to us by the careful concerns of many sensitive workers in the field, conveys the richness of the Feminine deity and Her transformative power. I believe that Snake Woman, although not the most regal or imposing of the Feminine deities in Navajo myth, holds a deeply "human" promise that the Feminine has a place and a function of immeasurable worth. She holds a knowledge that we have need of.

The complementarity of Feminine/Masculine, so pervasive in Navajo thought, so permeating all of life, may indeed be the singular complementarity which, if taken seriously, can make or break a world. The serpent carries for us a sense of knowing about things unknowable, about things lying deep under the things known.

The journey of Snake Woman is a paradigm of that journey to be taken by the Feminine in all of us, especially in women. It is the journey through darkness and death to rebirth and wholeness.

Theodotus, as quoted by the early church father, Clement of Alexandria, gave a description of *gnosis* which is a marvelous description of the Snake Woman god-journey. He said that gnosis was "the knowledge of who we were, what we have become, where we were, into what place we have been thrown, whither we are hastening, whence we are redeemed, what is birth, what is rebirth."

POSTLUDE

In manifold ways and through diverse wanderings of mythic tales I have tried to explore the Pueblo and Navajo people's ideas of and feelings about the Feminine. In doing this I have been drawn into doing at least five other things. I have had to examine myths of other peoples. I have looked into dreams and struggles of contemporary women and men.

In both myths and dreams I have seen revealed the human psyche's genius in weaving the mythic realm from inside its evolving Self — struggling to articulate what it itself is, what the cultural climate surrounding it is, and what are its perceptions of the Other, the more-than-itself Other.

I hope we have become somewhat more familiar with, and at ease in, the myths in the same manner as we grow more accustomed to our persons when the inside comes outside. Inevitably and finally, I have come to the place of realizing and emphasizing that the Feminine cannot exist alone any more than can the Masculine, either in us or in the larger meanings.

Granted a long historical period of Masculine dominance and a consequent cultural onesidedness, the answer cannot be merely to move into an equally long period of Feminine dominance. Such dominance has doubtless existed in certain periods of human prehistory and history — i.e., during times of paleolithic goddess cults as on Malta and Crete. However, our recorded human history shows more Masculine domination than Feminine domination. And it seems that the more technologically oriented we have become the more this one-sidedness has been true.

It is well to remind ourselves that all beings are not alike, although flowers, birds, fish, other "lower" animal species, are more alike within their ranks than human animal beings are. We have (although we make poor use of it) a much more complex and extendable consciousness. We have broader capacities for expression — ranging from Shakespeare to Marquis de Sade, from Madame Curie to Madame Pompadour.

Other animals (i.e., dogs and cats) dream — or at any rate show all measurable signs of dreaming except telling us what the dream content is. Only we humans can record, discuss, make books about, dreams. Only we human beings (so far) can tell of the mysteries of myth, of the strangely illumined dark reaches of our inner archetypal worlds behind the workaday places, can make mystery rites and ceremonies celebrating deities.

Only we human beings articulate ourselves in polarities, complementarities, opposites, all rocking back and forth on the fulcrum of "I." Often we are pushed and pulled by these polarities. Sometimes we choose bravely to "teeter" and "totter" because that makes a rhythm, a counting, like seasons, like deep breathing. The "I" can know and can know that it knows itself either as a "she-I" or a "he-I" — both as to physical characteristics and as to behaviors (some acquired, some archetypally patterned).

But further than that — and this is a giant step in insight — we human beings can know, and have set forth that knowing in our great religious myths and ceremonies, that Beginning Itself is a She-He. Or sometimes an It that becomes a She-He. This is an argument for the innate bipolarity in us and in deity.

There are many anthropologists, naturalists, biologists, psychologists (i.e., Eiseley, Doubzhansky, Jung, Teilhard de Chardin, Rachel Levy) who support the conviction that opposites and their rhythms are there in fact and from the beginning. The complexities of "instinct" — which is coming back into fashion since excellent demonstrations of its reality* — lend firm support to the assertion that the unconscious archetypal world of the human being has a much longer and more impressive history than the learned conscious world.

*For fuller discussion of this work, the reader is referred to *Spirit and Nature* (Bollingen Series XXX, No. 1, Pantheon Books, N.Y., 1954), especially to the articles "Biology and the Phenomenon of the Spirit," by Adolf Portmann, and "The Spirit of Psychology," by C.G. Jung; and to *Man and Transformation* (Bollingen Series XXX, No. 5, Pantheon Books, N.Y., 1964), especially to the article "Metamorphosis in Animals," by Portmann. There is also some excellent material in *The Myth of Meaning*, by Aniela Jaffe (Biblio. No. 40).

Feminine and Masculine belong first and deepest to the Other (whatever It is) than to the archetypal level of our being, and finally to the more conscious level. Our outer behavior is patterned on what goes on in depths below and beyond our immediate knowing far more than it is patterned on what we have "learned" from our environment. Both are operative, but the first is the more powerful, thrusting itself into the second in ways beyond our control.

There are somatic differences between male and female. There are also psychic differences based just as surely on the archetypal realm as are the differences between male and female in the lower animals. This is not to say that there are no "learned" behaviors that have become sex-linked, habitual, "correct." There are a great many. Some of these are being seen through and therefore altered, not without strife and pain. But the real psychic differences, resting both on the substrate of the unconscious (virtually "instinctual" and genetically coded, perhaps) and also on a transcendent otherness, must not be passed over. How a male human being works with the Masculine is different from how a female human being works with the Masculine. The same holds true for the Feminine.

There are certain archetypal structures which make the Masculine closer to the "natural" man — natural here meaning relatively unhurt by the cultural pressures — and make the Feminine similarly closer to the "natural" woman. Every human being must be related to both dimensions if personal wholeness and balance are being sought.

As we earth citizens approach our nadir it is possible that we can find a more all-inclusive way to interact with our world, each other, our inner selves, and the Other. This way presupposes the equal use of and the equal honoring of the Feminine and the Masculine in every person, in most of life's situations, and in the deity.

It does not mean that Feminine and Masculine are necessarily equal in any given situation. Sometimes Feminine is needed most, sometimes Masculine — just as sometimes we need a much deepened inhalation and at other times a fuller letting go of breath. It does mean that both are available to and need to be operative in every individual. As they are present always in deity.

We can discover (or activate) the Feminine aspects in our inner being by asking questions of ourselves. Am I able to flow, to be open to change? In myself? In outer situations? Can I encompass nature's rhythms? Other people's rhythms when they are different from mine? Do I really know what mine are? Can I encompass events as they come to (or at) me by enfolding them, taking them inward in love rather than pushing them away?

How much of the time is what I do inner-directed? Or just based on what I want? Am I compassionate towards myself? Towards others? Do I have the unstrained "quality of Mercy?" Where? How?

Can I permit things to happen? Can I *consciously choose* to let things happen? As different from abdicating? Am I as at home in earthy and/or watery modes (in others, in myself, in situations) as in airy and/or fiery ones? What modes do I like best in others? In art? In music?.

Do I let my sensorium lead me as much as my head? Can I be catlike? Childlike (not childish) in appreciating my senses? Am I as concerned with "communion" and relating as with their opposites? With reference to myself? To others? Do I see the asking and answering of these questions as a journey towards a deepened spiritual meaning and psychological maturity?

All of these questions can be answered with reference to the larger world. If we work at them fully, honestly, devotedly, we can begin to learn much about the Feminine in us. And friends can give us their opinions — if we've courage enough to ask. Writing out, painting out, using our bodies to act out, whatever of the Feminine we begin to find in ourselves — these are ways to see the dimensions more clearly.

Whether or not we consider ourselves religious, regardless of our upbringing, if we are in any way ponderers we ponder beginnings, we return to places before time. Very small children do this unselfconsciously in such questions as, "Way way before me or mommy or daddy or anything or anybody or my dog or anything, what was there?" This question has been "answered" in divergent ways mythically, and countless volumes have been filled with arguments about answers. Why is it a concern of ours here? Because the thousands of years of Judeo-Christian culture have been dominated by a He-God, which fact has tilted the scales far over on the Masculine side. It is not the purpose of this book to trace the long and complex history of why this has been so. (See Biblio No. 38.)

For myself I do not assume that all this was done by males with hostility towards females. It was not consciously "done" at all by anyone. It came about. It evolved. Creation myths grow as a culture grows, evolve as a culture evolves. Both move from the unconscious world to the conscious one. Different cultures have different creation myths. In a highly developed culture there will be a highly developed (albeit perhaps onesided) consciousness. Historically this tends to lead to the formation and entrenchment of castes — religious, political, scientific. This then leads to a raising of the Masculine to the superior place, although this has not been true everywhere, as we have seen in many myths.

In *Ecclesiasticus* 24:9, Wisdom — a She — says, "He created me from the beginning — before the world — and I shall never cease."

A contemporary poet, Babette Deutsch, in a moving modern hymn to the goddess Isis, says in poetry what prose can only approximate. She describes how we are like the limbs of the dismembered Osiris, scattered, fragmented, "beaten upon by the sea,/Unknowing, dying." And we call Isis to help us. "Where were you then, my sister, my soul?"

Isis sought for the scattered parts. "And you came, O soul, my sister,/Flying quick with compassion, the sleepless mother,/Unwearied bride." The dispersed parts were united, the lost members restored. But can we make it? the voice cries out. "Can we forgive and govern . . . ? On the horns of the/Savage dividing waters,/Can we endure?" The reply comes as unmistakable as a single clear and poignant oboe note:

> *Do not*
> *Speak, mother and bride, my sister:*
> *We that were*
> *Scattered, now are made one,*
> *We that were*
> *Parted, now are at peace.*
> *O do not*
> *Lay a lightest feather upon the scales*
> *Held in equipoise of triumphant stillness.*
> *Now, my sister, my soul, requited, remember*
> *As I, requited, foresee*
> *The workings of Evil, past and to come.*
> *Nor deny —*
> *Denial only is dying —*
> *This moment of union.* (21)

She — this Isis, this Changing Woman, this Snake Woman —whoever we name Her — let us be concerned that She will never cease. Let us hope that She — "my sister, my soul" — will forever help us to gather up our scattered parts and "requite" us at "this moment of union."

She, the Changing, ceaseless as the sea and liquid as the moon, eternally roaming in search of the dispersed and of the essential "communion" of us and of all humankind — She can be held and not held, heard and not heard, but felt always in the heart's central room if we but leave the door ajar lovingly. It is impossible to imagine life going forward without the presence of such greatness as She carries. How otherwise could we hear the small voices that speak to us out of silence? How otherwise could we honor the very

least of those who live within us? From what
other sources could we learn forgiveness and being forgiven? How would it be possible to be lovingly objective or objectively loving without a
She like one of these? In their hands the Feminine is raised to its finest and highest. Moreover,
it is we who must honor Her and Her earths and
seas. Our needs can be met only if we help Her.

The stone of a world lies helpless
till I come. The oil of a world
may light no lamp, may heal no hurt
until I come. Lofted with stars, sky
fills itself with breath to blow out
torches of a world unless I come.
An entire pregnant universe waits upon me.
A foundling, loveless, unillumined, can I
fulfill this burdened wish for renaissance
crushing against my courage (as do silent
and large-eyed entreaties of beasts)?
I am neither mistress nor master
of midnight labyrinths, but stumbler,
maladroit, subject as what I seek is
to that Other Who breathes and my voice
speaks, Who wearies and my body rests.

REFERENCES AND BIBLIOGRAPHY

1. Aeschylus. *The Eumenides*. Trans. by R. Lattimore. Chicago: University of Chicago Press, 1960.

2. Albright, William F. *Yahweh and the Gods of Canaan*. New York: Doubleday and Co., 1969.

3. Alexander, Harley Burr. *The World's Rim*. Lincoln: University of Nebraska Press, 1953.

4. Alexander, Hartley Burr, ed. *Mythology of All Races*. Vols. I-XIII, especially Vol. X. Boston: MacMillan Co., 1944; Archaeological Institute of America.

5. Bancroft, Hubert. *The Native Races of the Pacific States*. Vol. III. New York: Appleton Co., 1875.

6. Barbeau, Marius. *Haida Myths*. National Museum of Canada, Bulletin 127, 1953.

7. Berdyaev, Nicolas. *The Meaning of the Creative Act*. London: Gollancz, 1955.

8. *The Bible*, R.S.V. of Oxford Annotated. New York: Oxford University Press, 1973.

9. Bredon, Juliet, and Mitrophanow, Igor. *The Moon Year*. Shanghai: Kelly and Walsh, Ltd., 1927.

10. Brown, Joseph E. *The Sacred Pipe*. Norman: University of Oklahoma Press, 1953.

11. Burckhardt, Titus. *Alchemy*. London: Stuart and Watkins, 1967.

12. Burland, C.A. *The Gods of Mexico*. New York: Putnam, 1967.

13. Carrighar, Sally. *The Twilight Seas*. New York: Weybright and Talley, 1975.

14. Carson, Rachel. *The Edge of the Sea*. Boston: Houghton Mifflin Co., 1955.

15. Cirlot, J.W. *A Dictionary of Symbols*. New York: Philosophical Library, 1962.

16. Corbin, Henry. *"Mundus Imaginalis."* New York: *Spring*, 1972.

17. Courlander, Harold. *The Fourth World of the Hopis.* Greenwich, Connecticut: Fawcett Premier Books, 1971.

18. Cousteau, Jacques-Ives. *The Silent World.* New York: Ballantine Books, 1955.

19. Cousteau, Jacques-Ives. *The Living Sea.* New York: Ballantine Books, 1973.

20. Danielou, Alain. *Hindu Polytheism.* Bollingen Series LXXIII. New York: Pantheon Books, 1964.

21. Deutsch, Babette. *Coming of Age.* Bloomington: Indiana University Press, 1959.

22. Doubzhansky, Theodosius. *The Biology of Ultimate Concern.* New York: The New American Library, Inc., 1967.

23. Eisley, Loren. *The Immense Journey.* New York: Vintage Books, 1957.

24. Eisley, Loren. *The Night Country.* New York: Scribner's and Sons, 1971.

25. Eliade, Mircea. *Patterns in Comparative Religion.* New York: Sheed and Ward, 1958.

26. Eliot, T.S. *The Family Reunion.* New York: Harcourt, Brace and Co., 1939.

27. Eliot, T.S. *The Cocktail Party.* New York: Harcourt, Brace and Co., 1950.

28. Elsworthy, F.T. *The Evil Eye.* New York: Julian Press, 1958.

29. Goetz, D., and Morley, S.G., Trans. *Popol Vuh.* Norman: University of Oklahoma Press, 1950.

30. Haile, Fr. Berard, and Wheelwright, Mary. *Emergence Myth.* Santa Fe, New Mexico: Museum of Navajo Ceremonial Art, Inc., 1949.

31. Haile, Fr. Berard; Oakes, Maud; Newcomb, F.J.; and Wyman, Leland C. *Beautyway, A Navajo Ceremonial.* Bollingen Series LIII. New York: Pantheon Books, 1957.

32. Hannah, Barbara. *Striving for Wholeness.* New York: G.P. Putnam's Sons, 1971.

33. Henderson, J.L. and Oakes, Maud. *The Wisdom of the Serpent.* New York: George Braziller, Inc., 1963.

34. Hoijer, Harry. *Texts of the Navajo Creation Chant.* Trans. by M.C. Wheelwright and D.P. McAllester. Cambridge: Museum of Harvard University, 1950.

35. Hooke, S.N., ed. *Myth, Ritual and Kingship.* London: Oxford Press, 1958.

36. Hooke, S.N., ed. *Myth and Ritual*. London: Oxford Press, 1933.

37. Howes, Elizabeth Boyden. *Intersection and Beyond*. San Francisco: Guild for Psychological Studies, 1971.

38. Howes, Elizabeth, and Moon, Sheila. *The Choicemaker*. Wheaton, Illinois: Theosophical Publishing House. Quest Book, 1977.

39. Jacobi, Jolande. *The Psychology of Jung*. New Haven, Connecticut: Yale University Press, 1943.

40. Jaffe, Aniela. *The Myth of Meaning*. New York: Putnam's Sons, 1971.

41. James, E.O. *The Cult of the Mother Goddess*. London: Thames and Hudson, 1959.

42. James, H.C. *The Hopi Indians*. Idaho: Caxton Printers, 1956.

43. Jung, C.G. *Collected Works*. Bollingen Series XX. New York: Pantheon Books.

44. Jung, C.G. *The Archetypes and the Collective Unconscious*. Bollingen Series XX. New York: Pantheon Books, 1959.

45. Jung, C.G. *Psychology and Alchemy*. Bollingen Series XX. New York: Pantheon Books, 1953.

46. Jung, C.G. *Mysterium Coniunctionis.* Bollingen Series XX. New York: Pantheon Books, 1963.

47. Jung, C.G. *et al. Man and His Symbols.* New York: Doubleday and Co., 1964.

48. Jung, Emma. *Animus and Anima.* New York: Analytical Psychology Club of New York, 1957.

49. Kluckhorn, Clyde, and Leighton, Dorothea. *The Navajo.* Cambridge: Harvard University Press, 1946.

50. Kramer, Noah. *Mythologies of the Ancient World.* Chicago, Illinois: Quadrangle Books, 1961.

51. LeGuin, Ursula K. *The Dispossessed.* New York: Harper and Row, 1974.

52. Levy, G. Rachel. *Religious Conceptions of the Stone Age.* Harper Torchbook, 1963.

53. Link, Margaret Schevill. "From the Desk of Washington Matthews." *Junior America Folklore.* Vol. 72, No. 290.

54. Long, Charles H. *Alpha.* New York: Collier Books, 1969.

55. Maringer, Johannes. *The Gods of Prehistoric Man.* New York: A Knopf, 1960.

56. Marriott, Alice, and Rachlin, Carol K. *American Indian Mythology*. New York: Crowell Co., 1968.

57. Matthews, Washington. *Manuscript No. 456*. Santa Fe: Museum of Navajo Ceremonial Art.

58. Mendelsohn, E., ed. *Religions of the Ancient Near East*. New York: Liberal Arts Press, 1955.

59. Miller, Henry. *The Smile at the Foot of the Ladder*. New York: New Directions Press, 1958.

60. Moon, Sheila. *A Magic Dwells*. Middletown, Connecticut: Wesleyan University Press, 1970.

61. Murray, Margaret. *The God of the Witches*. New York: Oxford, 1952.

62. Neihardt, John. *Black Elk Speaks*. Lincoln: University of Nebraska Press, 1961.

63. Neumann, Erich. *Origins and History of Consciousness*. Bollingen Series XLII. New York: Pantheon Books, 1954.

64. Neumann, Erich. *The Great Mother*. Bollingen Series XLII. New York: Pantheon Books, 1955.

65. Neumann, Erich. *Depth Psychology and A New Ethic*. New York: Putnam, 1969.

229

66. Newcomb, Franc J.; Fisher, Stanley; and
    Wheelwright, Mary C. *A Study of Navajo
    Symbolism*, Vol. XXXII, No. 3, Papers of
    the Peabody Museum. Cambridge: Har-
    vard University Press, 1956.

67. Newcomb, Franc J. *Navajo Folk Tales.*
    Santa Fe: Museum of Navajo Ceremonial
    Art, Inc., 1967.

68. Nicholson, Irene. *Mexican and Central
    American Mythology*. London: Paul
    Hamlin, Ltd., 1967.

69. Nicholson, Irene. *Firefly in the Night.*
    London: Faber and Faber, 1959.

70. O'Brien, Tom. "Marrying Malthus and
    Marx." *Environmental Action*. Vol. 7, No.
    8, Aug. 30, 1975.

71. Oakes, Maud, and Campbell, Joseph.
    Where the Two Came to Their Father. Boll-
    ingen Series I. New York: Pantheon
    Books, 1943.

72. Ostrovski-Sachs, Margaret. *From Conver-
    sations with C.G. Jung*. Zurich: Juris
    Druck, 1971.

73. Pelgrin, Mark. *And A Time To Die*. Lon-
    don: Routledge and Kegan Paul, 1961;
    Wheaton, Illinois: Re-Quest Books, 1976.

74. Perry, John W. *Lord of the Four Quarters.*
    New York: Braziller, 1966.

75. Phillips, Dorothy B., and Howes, Elizabeth B. *The Choice Is Always Ours.* Rev. and Abridged. New York: Pyramid; Wheaton, Illinois: Re-Quest Books, 1975.

76. Reichard, Gladys. *Navajo Religion.* Vol. XVIII, 1st ed. Bollingen Series. New York: Pantheon Press, 1950.

77. Reichard, Gladys. *Spider Woman.* Glorieta, New Mexico: Rio Grande Press, Inc., 1968.

78. Rilke, Rainer Maria. *Translations from Rilke* by C.W. MacIntyre. Berkeley: University of California Press, 1941.

79. Rilke, Rainer Maria. *Letters, 1892-1910.* New York: W.W. Norton, 1945.

80. Sandner, Donald. *Navajo Symbols of Healing.* New York: Harcourt, Brace, Jovanovich, 1979.

81. Sarton, May. *Cloud, Stone, Sun, Vine.* New York: W. W. Norton, 1961.

82. Sarton, May. *Collected Poems, 1930-1973.* New York: W.W. Norton, 1974.

83. Stephen, Alexander. *Hopi Journal,* Vol. I. New York: Columbia University Press, 1936.

84. Stevenson, M.C. "The Zuni Indians," *B.A.E.* 23 d Ann. Rep. (1905).

85. Summers, Montague. *Malleus Maleficarum*. London: Pushkin Press, 1887.

86. Teilhard de Chardin, Pierre. *The Phenomenon of Man.*. New York: Harper and Row, 1959.

87. Thompson, Stith. *Tales of the North American Indians*. Bloomington: Indiana University Press, 1971.

88. Trinick, John. *The Fire-Tried Stone*. London: Wordens of Cornwall, Ltd., and Stuart and Watkins, Ltd., 1967.

89. Tyler, H.A. *Pueblo Gods and Myths*. Norman: University of Oklahoma Press, n.d.

90. Underhill, Ruth M. *Singing for Power*. Berkeley: Univ. of California Press, 1938.

91. Von Franz, Marie-Louise. *Aurora Consurgens*. Bollingen Series LXXVII. New York: Pantheon, 1966.

92. Waters, Frank. *Book of the Hopi*. New York: Viking Press, 1963.

93. Wickes, Frances. *The Inner World of Choice*. New York: Harper and Row, 1963.

94. Wilhelm, R., Trans. *I Ching*. Bollingen Series XIX. New York: Pantheon, 1950.

95. Williams, Charles. *Descent Into Hell.* New York: Pellagrini and Cudahy, 1949.

96. Williams, Charles. *The Greater Trumps.* London: Faber, 1932.

97. Wyman, Leland C. *BlessingWay.* Tucson: University of Arizona Press, 1970.

98. Wyman, Leland C. *The Red Antway of the Navajo.* Santa Fe, New Mexico: Museum of Navajo Ceremonial Art, Inc., 1965.

99. Wyman, Leland C. *The Sandpaintings of the Kayenta Navajo.* University of New Mexico Publ. in Anthropology, No. 7, 1952.

100. Wyman, Leland C. "The Religion of the Navajo Indians." *Forgotten Religions.* Ed. by V. Ferm. New York: Philosophical Library, n.d.

101. Zimmer, Heinrich. "The Chakras of Kundalini Yoga." *Spring,* 1975. New York: Analytical Psychology Club of New York.